Just Green It!

by LISA and RON BERES

RUNNING PRESS

PHILADELPHIA · LONDON

9 8 7 6 5 4 3 2 1
Digit on the right indicates the number of this printing

Library of Congress Control Number: 2009939336
ISBN 978-0-7624-3877-8

Edited by Geoffrey Stone
Typography: Berkeley & Frutiger

Running Press Book Publishers
2300 Chestnut Street
Philadelphia, PA 19103-4371

Visit us on the web!
www.runningpress.com

Visit them on the web:
www.GreenNest.com

For 15% off on valuable green products exclusively at www.GreenNest.com, use coupon code:

#6GN82245

In loving memory of Genevieve Kroviak

TABLE OF CONTENTS

PREFACE

TO GREEN OR NOT TO GREEN? That was the question. However, in today's day and age, regardless of the unstable economy, making "green" choices and living a healthier lifestyle is becoming less of a luxury and more of a norm. Researchers have even predicted a shift in future trends that "non-green" will not survive. Good news? If everything were as it seemed, it would most definitely be good news. However, in this recent surge of "greenifying" our world and marketplace, the line between what is and what appears, has become blurred, leaving the consumer to feel overwhelmed, bombarded, and, in many cases, deceived. The need to make a profit is not a crime, but at what point is the crime committed when profit supersedes integrity? Greenwashing has taken the marketplace by storm to the point that watchdog groups and websites have evolved to keep us abreast of these false advertising culprits. The average consumer must go far beyond reading a label. We now require an education that includes green definitions and product comparisons to keep us safe from the eight-legged marketers' colorful web of names and terms that sound, look, or even taste healthy and environmentally friendly. In nearly every purchasing decision you may ask yourself if the short-term savings are really worth the long-term price tag on our health and planet.

Everything in our lifestyle—what we eat, touch, wear, and use to furnish our homes—is linked to our health and well-being. Are genetics loading the gun and environment and lifestyle choices pulling the trigger as many have previously thought? Lisa certainly believes so. She became very ill from living in a toxic environment created by everyday, trusted products. It was only through Lisa's diligent research and a need for the truth that she discovered that products are not always what they seem. We have allowed a society with an "innocent until proven guilty" mentality in everything from pesticides and plastics to lead, tobacco, asbestos, and pharmaceuticals. In the U.S., chemicals are typically regulated *after* studies indicate potential harm exists and a regulatory review is conducted.

With so many untested and unregulated harmful chemicals in the products that surround us, it's no wonder that people get sick. Yet, with so little testing and regulation most of us are not informed enough to know the cause. Instead, Lisa and many others run through the gamut of doctor visits, treatments, and medications to mask symptoms. As Gloria Steinem put it best ". . . *Who profits from causing, detecting, and treating cancer? Why do we hear so much about the search for a cure, and so little about preventing cancer in the first place?"*

Through the highways of cyberspace, information has become ubiquitous. You might think it's easy to make educated choices, but who really has time in our faced-paced, twenty-first century, technology-thriving world to do all of the researching? Fear not, there is a green light at the end of this tunnel. We have deciphered fact from fiction to inform and educate you on how to live a healthier lifestyle while empowering you, the consumer, to exercise not just your voice, but your purchasing power. Demand better products, and they will become more readily available. Don't settle for untested or unregulated goods for you, your family, and our planet. You can—and you do—make a difference!

Be the change you want to see in the world.
— MAHATMA GANDHI

THE THREE SIDES OF THE GREEN TRIANGLE: THE THREE "Rs," ENERGY EFFICIENCY, AND INDOOR AIR QUALITY

THE THREE "Rs"

REDUCE

Use paper towels with smaller tear sheets, not extra-thick and super-sized sheets.

The best-selling brands of paper towels are made from virgin tree pulp and then bleached white with chlorine, which pollutes the air and water. Look for towels that come in smaller sheets so you use less for each job.

Use glass storage containers, not plastic storage bags or wrap.

While plastic storage bags and wrap make storing leftovers and packing lunches easy, they are hard on the environment. These plastic products are not commonly accepted for recycling and are designed for a single use and then a trip to the landfill. While it is tempting to re-use them, it's not a good idea because they can leach chemicals into your food. This is especially true if they are used to reheat the food. Some plastic wraps are made with PVC, which poses health and environmental risks, so reusing those is particularly dangerous. Instead, buy glass containers with tops. These containers are generally thick, durable glass and come in all sizes and shapes so they are convenient for food storage as well as taking with you on the go.

Opt out of junk mail, don't just recycle.

Junk mail is not only annoying, but it also can be harmful to the environment by promoting additional waste and utilizing precious resources. Choose to reduce and eliminate direct mail by "opting out" of receiving both junk mail and catalogues. Visit these sites to have your name removed from future mailings—your desk (and planet) will thank you!

www.catalogchoice.org
www.greendimes.com
www.41pounds.org
www.stopthejunkmail.com
www.DMAchoice.org

Use Priority Mail, not next-day or second-day air shipping.

Sometimes being organized can help you live greener. Just allowing enough time for a package to reach its destination via ground mail can help fight global warming. Ground shipping is 6 times more fuel-efficient than air shipping.

Use dishwasher, not washing by hand.

Low-tech hand washing may seem like the greener choice over automatic dishwashing. The machines are made from plastic and metals and require electricity to run. However, the average late model dishwasher uses 3.5 gallons of water per load. Do the same load by hand and you'll run through 15 to 16 gallons. To reduce the amount of energy used by your dishwasher, it is important to make informed choices. First, make sure the dishwasher is full so you can run it less often. Skip the "Heat Dry" and "Pre-rinse" options and let the dishes air dry. If it's time to replace your dishwasher, choose an Energy-Star-certified dishwasher to ensure that it's energy efficient.

Use electric lawnmower or push mower, not gas powered.

The Environmental Protection Agency (EPA) estimates that 54 million Americans are out mowing their lawns every weekend and use 800 million gallons of gas to do it. Gas mowers pollute 10% to 35% more than the average car, and experts estimate that homeowners routinely spill thousands of gallons of gas as they fill up their tanks. To reduce your lawn care pollution, get an electric mower, or try a non-motorized push mower with spinning blades for small yard.

DISPOSABLE CUTLERY

Green it!

PRESERVE® CUTLERY

THE GOOD
Preserve Plastic™ is BPA, phthalate, and melamine free.

THE GREEN
By choosing products that are 100% recycled such as Preserve by Recycline, you help save Mother Earth's energy and natural resources. All Preserve products are designed to stay out of landfills because they are dishwasher safe and can withstand hundreds of uses. Recycle when you are finished with them.

THE CONVENIENT TRUTH
Look for products manufactured in the U.S.—they require less energy to transport.

Sage Advice
Some plastics contain BPA, Bisphenol A, an industrial chemical used to make polycarbonate plastic and epoxy resins. BPA has been associated with health disorders and diseases that include breast and prostate cancer and infertility.

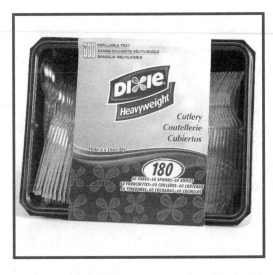

Sage Advice

Based on a Life Cycle Assessment, (LCA) by PE Americas' which measures a products impact from the beginning to the end, Preserve's products use at least 54% less water, 64% less greenhouse gas, 75% less oil, 48% less coal, 77% less natural gas, and 46% less electricity than virgin polypropylene.

Skip it!

PLASTIC DISPOSABLE CUTLERY

THE UGLY

According to Earth911.org, the U.S. throws out enough disposal dinnerware every year to *circle the equator 300 times.*

THE INCONVENIENT TRUTH

To reduce environmental impact, avoid items colored with titanium dioxide. Opt for those made from #5 polypropylene plastic (safe food-grade material) made with colors approved by the FDA and recycled content.

DISPOSABLE PLATES AND CUPS

Green it!

BARE™ BY SOLO®
PLATES AND CUPS

THE GOOD

Bare by Solo is the industry's first line of eco-forward™ single-use products for restaurants and consumers made using recycled, recyclable, compostable, or annually renewable materials. The square plates are made from sugar cane, the tan cups from corn, and the clear cups from recycled plastic!

THE GREEN

Going green doesn't mean saying goodbye to convenience items.

Ron's Green $$ Tip

Recycle. Earn points. Go shopping! If it is available in your city, sign up at www.recyclebank.com to earn points every time you recycle!

THE CONVENIENT TRUTH

Bare works with Keep America Beautiful™ and the Great American Cleanup™, which utilizes millions of volunteers each spring across the country to clean-up, green-up, fix-up, and beautify their communities.

Sage Advice

A smart choice for plates is bamboo. It is a fast growing, abundant, woody, perennial, evergreen plant that can grow 3 to 4 feet in one day! It can even be used for construction of houses, bridges, fences, and furniture due to the durability of its short fibers.

Skip it!

DISPOSABLE PAPER PLATES AND CUPS

THE UGLY

According to the Environmental Protection Agency, 75% of American's trash can be recycled, but only about 25% actually is.

THE INCONVENIENT TRUTH

In 2006, 6.5 million trees were cut to produce 16 billion paper coffee cups!
 Beware of the coating in most paper cups. Polyethylene is used for insulation but prevents them from being recycled. Look instead for those coated in PLA - Polylatic acid made from plant sugars and recyclable.

REUSE

Compost instead of mulching

Composting enables you to reduce the amount of garbage your family produces and improve your landscaping at the same time. Once your food scraps and yard trimmings decompose, spread the compost around your plants, as you would mulch. The compost helps keep the moisture in and protect the plants. The nutrients from your compost will feed your plants and improve your soil. Plus, you save money, resources, and packaging by not buying new bags of mulch each year.

Sage Advice

Electric lawn mowers produce less than 1% of the smog-contributing carbon monoxide that gas mowers put out and 1/9000th the hydrocarbons. They produce 6 pounds less carbon dioxide per typical use. The average electric mower is also considerably quieter than its gas equivalent, and 10-year operating costs are less than half those of gas mowers, making up for the higher initial cost.

   Source: National Geographic Green Guide: Moving without Grass

Use microfiber towels, not paper towels or disposable wipes

Reducing your paper towel use can help conserve trees and cut down on the pollution produced in the bleaching process. Reducing or eliminating synthetic wipes from your cleaning kit is even better since they will not readily biodegrade in the landfills. The next time you plan to use disposable wipes, consider that 83,000 tons of disposable wipes wind up in North American landfills every year.

Microfiber towels can do anything paper towels or wipes can do, and usually microfiber does it better. Microfiber is more absorbent than paper towels, and it also catches and holds dust instead of scattering it. Buy several so you can throw them in the wash and grab another as you clean.

Sage Advice

Get to know your triangles! These recycling rating numbers, called the SPI (Society of Plastic Industry) Resin Identification Code, are located inside the triangle and indicate the material used. They are not only essential for recycling efforts but offer information from a health perspective. You can typically find the following plastics for the following usages.

#1 polyethylene terephthalate (PET, PETE): is used in soft drink and single-use water bottles.

#2 high-density polyethylene (HDPE): is used in milk bottles, liquid detergent bottles and shampoo bottles.

#3 polyvinyl chloride (V, PVC): is used in found in meat wrap, cooking oil bottles,and pipes.

#4 Low-density polyethylene (LDPE): is used in cling wrap, grocery bags, sandwich bags.

#5 Polypropylene (PP): is used in Yogurt cups, ketchup bottles, cloudy plastic water bottle, and yogurt cups/tubs.

#6 Polystyrene (PS): disposable coffee cups and clam-shell take-out containers.

#7 or PC, and polylactide, or PLA, plastics made from renewable resources as well as newer plastics labeled "BPA free" and include baby bottles, some reusable water bottles, and stain-resistant food-storage containers.

SHOPPING BAGS

Green it!

REUSABLE, RECYCLED FOLDABLE TOTE

THE GOOD
Grab a reusable blue bag from Ikea for only 59 cents! As an extra incentive to do so, Ikea now charges 5 cents per disposable bag and donates the money to charity.

THE GREEN
Increase marine life by decreasing plastic waste.
- 143 known marine species (ex. sea turtles) have become entwined in plastic debris
- 177 known marine species have consumed plastic debris

THE CONVENIENT TRUTH
Take a reusable cloth bag to the store. If not for you, do it for sea life. Of all known species of sea turtles, 86% have had problems of entanglement or ingestion of marine debris.

Sage Advice
The Whole Foods reusable tote, designed by Sheryl Crow, is made of 80% post-consumer recycled plastic bottles and supports the Natural Resources Defense Council's (NRDC) Simple Steps program.

Sage Advice

It's been estimated that a plastic bag takes one thousand years to decompose. Does this mean paper bags are more environmentally friendly than plastic? Although recycled more often, the production of paper sacks produce 70% more air pollutants and take up more space in the landfill than plastic bags!

More than 14 million trees were chopped down to manufacture the 10 billion paper grocery bags used in the U.S. in 1999!

Skip it!

PAPER OR PLASTIC BAGS

THE UGLY
Many grocery stores have recycle bins for shopping bags, however only 10 to 15% of paper and 1 to 3% of plastic bags are recycled!

THE INCONVENIENT TRUTH
An estimated 500 billion to 1 trillion plastic bags are used annually worldwide. That's more than one million per minute!

Approximately 100 billion plastic shopping bags a year are added to America's landfills! Less than 5% of shoppers in America are using canvas, cotton, or mesh bags.

TO-GO CUPS

Green it!

STARBUCKS®
TO-GO COLD CUP

THE GOOD
The Starbucks To-Go Cold Cup is BPA Free. BPA is an endocrine disruptor that binds to the body's natural receptor sites and is linked to risk of reproductive, neuronal and/ or immunological damage.

- -

THE GREEN
The To-Go Cold Cup by Starbucks Coffee is double walled, dishwasher safe, and recommended for cold beverages only. Drink responsibly!

- -

THE CONVENIENT TRUTH
If forced to choose, opt for plastic instead of Styrofoam as it can at least be recycled. Three million tons of Styrofoam are generated each year in the United States—most of that ending up in landfills.

- -

Ron's Green $$ Tip
Starbucks locations offer customers a $0.10 discount when you use your own reusable cups. In 2006, customers took advantage of this offer more than 17 million times, preventing 674,000 pounds of paper from going to the landfill.

Mother Knows Best
Conventional cups are made from petroleum-based plastics, which use up the Earth's resources.

Skip it!

DISPOSABLE PLASTIC COFFEE CUPS

THE UGLY
Chemical additives are added to plastic to give flexibility, flame resistance, color or softness. These chemicals, (monomers) can leach out of plastics and into your food or drink depending on type of plastic and condition/wear.

THE INCONVENIENT TRUTH
Some additives in plastics mimic the action of hormones like estrogen which in turn make them man-made endocrine disruptors or xenoestrogens.

PAPER COFFEE CUPS

Green it!

I AM NOT A PAPER CUP

"I am not a paper cup..."
THERMAL PORCELAIN CUP WITH SILICONE LID

THE GOOD

Starbucks claims if 50 customers at each location used reusable mugs, they would save 150,000 cups per day, reducing waste by 1.7 million pounds of paper per year.

THE GREEN

According to Coffee-statistics.com, Americans alone consume 400 million cups of coffee per day—that's *146 billion cups* of coffee per year.

THE CONVENIENT TRUTH

The "I Am Not a Paper Cup" looks just like the modern to-go cup, but can be reused. It is both dishwasher and microwave safe and holds up to 10 ounces. Most important, it keeps paper cups out of landfills!

Sage Advice

According to a Life Cycle Analysis (LCA) of paper vs. ceramic by the Dutch Ministry of Environment, a ceramic cup reaps energy, pollution, and waste savings after long-term usage. (This shouldn't be a problem since they are designed for a long, durable life. It can be used well over 3,000 times.)

Mother Knows Best!

Starbucks to-go hot cups utilize 10% PCF fiber. Though no match to the benefits of a reusable cup, the Environmental Defense's Paper Calculator, www.papercalculator.org, states that customer usage of the PFC fiber cups has resulted in the company's significant reduction in the amount of wood use by 11,300 tons—the equivalent of 78,000 trees—in the first year alone.

Skip it!

DISPOSABLE PAPER COFFEE CUPS

THE UGLY
Wanna find out how much waste you are accumulating with your disposable cups of joe? Visit the Coffee Calculator at www. dzignism.com/projects/coffee.waste/ to find out

----

THE INCONVENIENT TRUTH
By choosing reusable ceramic or glass cups over disposable cups, you help prevent approximately 86 to 88 tons of solid waste from entering the landfill over a ceramic or glass cup's lifetime, according to a Report of the Alliance for Environmental Innovation Joint Task Force by the Starbucks Coffee Company.

RECYCLE

Use only recyclable "good" plastics.

Plastics are made from petroleum, a nonrenewable resource, and can contain toxins that leach into your food or drink. It's a good idea to reduce your use of plastic wherever possible. But when you do buy plastic bottles or containers, check the number on the bottom first and make sure they're recyclable.

GREEN THESE:

#1 PET, #2 HDPE, #4 LDPE and #5 PP: Plastics marked #1 are safe and widely accepted by municipal recyclers. Containers marked #2 are very commonly accepted by municipal recycling programs. Check your city's policy for recycling #4 and #5 containers.

NOT THESE:

#3 PVC, #6 PS and #7 PC: Plastics marked #3 should be avoided as much as possible. PVC contains chemicals that can damage your hormonal system and cause cancer. It is not recyclable and leaches heavy metals in the landfill. Plastics marked #6 and #7 also pose health risks and are not commonly accepted by recyclers.

Use rainwater catchment, not the garden hose.

While some people in the world can't get enough water to drink or bathe, Americans pour about 8 billion gallons of water a day on their lawns and landscaping. You can make a difference by setting up a rainwater catchment system to collect water off your roof. The systems are easy to build and, depending on where you live, may be enough to keep your yard watered without ever having to turn on the hose. You can use a 55-gallon wine or food barrel or a simple 5-gallon bucket and a gutter connection with a leaf and mosquito screen. An optional charcoal filter can be used to remove rooftop contaminants. Check your city to verify if rebates are available.

Use Recycle Bank, not the garbage can.

If recycling seems difficult or a hassle, you might want to raise the personal stakes for filling up your recycling bin instead of your trash can. Join Recycle Bank (www.recyclebank.com). You get points for every pound you recycle. You can then redeem those points for everything from a free latte to a percentage off your bill at Target or Petco.

Use Google, not the Yellow Pages.

Phone books are still not widely recyclable, but the good news is that they are also becoming obsolete. These days you can find any number you need using Google. However, just because you don't use phonebooks, doesn't mean they'll stop coming. Call the company to opt-out.

Purchase minimally packaged goods, not over-packaged goods.

Whenever you purchase something, consider the packaging that you'll be bringing home just to dump in the recycling bin or trash. If you're choosing between two products, choose the one with less packaging. Close the recycling loop by supporting manufacturers who use recycled materials in their packaging or who eliminate the packaging all together.

Recycle your own printer paper instead of using new paper.

Keep a bin next to your printer for used paper that has only been printed on one side. This is the paper to use when printing out documents that don't need to be on pristine paper, such as directions or recipes. Once you start doing this, it's easy to see how little of what we print actually needs to be on new paper. When you do buy printer paper, you can go to www.thegreenoffice.com to buy Postconsumer Waste (PCW) recycled paper.

Recycle your carpet instead of filling up the dumps.

If you're about to remove or replace your carpeting, think twice before you just have it hauled away to the landfill. It's estimated that nearly 5 billion pounds of carpeting end up in the landfills each year. Instead, donate or sell any carpet or area rugs that are still in good condition. For carpeting that is not in good condition, go to www.carpetrecovery.org to find out if there's a carpet recycling center near you.

Turn your old athletic shoes into play surfaces instead of throwing them out.

You can send your old stinky athletic shoes to Nike (www.nikereuseashoe.com), and they'll recycle them. The shoes become "Nike Grind," which is a material used for playgrounds, basketball courts, school tracks, and other play surfaces. Even better, the program is not restricted to Nike shoes—the program will accept any brand as long as they don't have cleats.

Use your shower filter cartridge contents for the garden instead of tossing them.

You can recycle some shower filters yourself. Just poke a hole in the screen and empty the cartridge in the garden. Then place the plastic in the recycling bin.

Ron's Green $$ Tip
Bottled water can costs hundreds and even thousands of times more per gallon than tap water. Save money with a home filtration system and reuse your containers.

ENERGY EFFICIENCY

Use Energy-Star appliances, not older appliances.

Even if your old appliances are still working fine, you may want to consider upgrading to Energy-Star-certified new models. That's because your old machines may be wasting energy and water every time you use them. That can add up in your utility bills, but also in the cost to the environment. Go to the Energy Star website (www.energystar.gov) to find certified models. You can also find out about tax credits and rebates that will make upgrading even more affordable.

Use the Hymini, not wall sockets for charging your personal electronics.

The Hymini (www.hymini.com) is a small but powerful gadget that can convert the wind and the sun's rays into power for all your personal electronics. You only need a wind speed of 9 mph, but can use up to 40 mph to generate power. They even sell a Bike Holder Package

so you can cheat and create your own wind.

Use the sleep mode instead of turning your computer off.

Some experts recommend setting computers to sleep mode after 5 minutes of idle time. Why? Desktop computers can cause 1,500 pounds of carbon dioxide a year; by enabling sleep mode you can reduce your energy consumption by up to 70%.

Sage Advice
Laptop computers use about half the energy of a tower.

Use energy efficient window shades, not PVC or metal shades.

Don't throw your money out the window! According to the U.S. Department of Energy, 10% to 25% of heating and cooling costs are lost through windows. Look for an energy-efficient shade like the Duette Architella from Hunter Douglas. They have a unique honeycomb-within-honeycomb design that can reduce heat loss by 50%. More air pockets mean greater insulation than traditional honeycomb shades.

Use a dual flush toilet, not the standard ones.

Standard toilets use nearly 3 gallons of water with every flush. Switching to a dual flush toilet can save 67% of that water. These eco-friendly toilets have two buttons that give you the power to choose exactly how big a flush you need. Since most trips to the bathroom don't require a powerful flush, the water savings is dramatic.

Use front loading, not top loading washing machines

It's important to replace old top loaders with Energy-Star-certified new front loaders as soon as possible. Although they're generally more expensive, front-loading models circulate clothes in a shallower pool of water, using less water and heat, and saving money in the long run. For example, replacing a pre-1994 washer can save a family up to $110 a year on utility bills.

Use cold or warm water, not hot water when washing clothes.

The next step to greening your laundry is to change your washer's temperature settings. Simply switching from washing in hot to warm can cut your energy use by half.

Use a dryer with moisture sensor or line dry, not an exhaust vent.

Dryers are the second biggest energy hog in your home, so it's important to make the most of whatever energy saving features they offer. Look for models that have a moisture sensor in the drum, as opposed to in the exhaust vent. A drum sensor will shut off a little sooner, saving slightly more energy. However, since dryers consume so much energy, line drying or hanging your clothes on a rack is a better option.

Use a high efficiency gas or tankless water heater, not standard electric models.

Tankless water heaters heat only the water you're using when you're using it instead of wasting energy to heat up more water than you need at any given time. Since heating water accounts for a third of your total energy bill, it's a good idea to switch to a more efficient water heater.

Sage Advice

The government estimates that tankless water heaters can save homeowners between 45 and 60% of water heating energy and up to $1,800 a year when compared to standard, minimum-efficiency heaters.

Source: National Geographic's *Green Guide*

Use fireplace inserts or a late-model wood stove, not a wood fireplace.

Wood-burning fireplaces without inserts and older model wood stoves may feel warm and cozy when you're in front of them, but they can actually take away more heat from your home than they contribute. Take a few steps back from the fireplace and you'll see what we mean. Plus, these cozy fires are major sources of pollution. Simply upgrading to an EPA-certified insert or a newer model woodstove can reduce your heating bills by nearly 40% and clean up your fireplace pollution by about 70%. If just 20 families made the switch to cleaner and more efficient fireplaces, there would be a ton less particulate matter pollution released into the air each year.

THERMOSTAT

Green it!

HONEYWELL® PROGRAMMABLE THERMOSTAT

THE GOOD
There are three types of programmable thermostats designed to fit your daily schedule—choose the one that best suits your needs and look for the Energy Star Label which meet strict energy efficiency guidelines set by the EPA and U.S. Department of Energy.

THE GREEN
A few settings can equal savings—$180 a year, in fact, if homeowners properly set their programmable thermostats and maintain those settings.

CONVENIENT TRUTH
Americans saved enough energy in 2008 alone to avoid greenhouse gas emissions equivalent to those from 29 million cars—all while saving $19 billion on their utility bills by using Energy Star!

Ron's Green $$ Tip
Wanna save about a third off you energy bill while also helping the planet? Energy efficient choices will help reduce greenhouse gas emissions while saving you green!

Skip it!
HONEYWELL® NON-PROGRAMMABLE THERMOSTAT

THE UGLY
Heating & cooling costs making you sweat? The average household spends more than $2,200 a year on energy bills according to Energy Star.

THE INCONVENIENT TRUTH
Every time you flip on a light switch, or turn on the TV, or turn the heat up and the air down, you are emitting carbon dioxide into the atmosphere and contributing to global warming. That's because most electrical production is fueled by coal-burning power plants, one of the world's biggest sources of carbon emissions—and a leading cause of global warming.

Sage Advice
You can calculate the savings using the Programmable Thermostat Calculator! A long URL, but a smaller bill is worth the effort. This was designed by the Department of Energy and the EPA to give you a Life Cycle Cost Estimate. Go to the site www.energystar.gov/index.cfm?c=thermostats.pr _thermostats and click on "savings calculator" in the resources section.

INDOOR AIR QUALITY

Test your air, don't guess.

The EPA deems poor indoor air quality one of the top five environmental risks the United States faces today. Contamination can come from a variety of sources, but now it is possible for air samples to be taken in the home and evaluated by a microbiology lab for accurate results. These home kits can test for molds, carcinogenic fibers like fiberglass or asbestos, formaldehyde, dander, pollen, bacteria, dust, and dust mites. Once you know what is polluting your indoor air, you can devise a more effective strategy to clean it.

While you're at it, you can test to see if your water is safe and if any toys, paint, or imported goods contain lead. To test all three, get a Home Detox Green Toolbox (www.Home DetoxGreenToolbox.com).

Use windows with fans, not air-conditioning.

Unlike air conditioning units, window fans use very little energy. To get the best results place the fans in windows that face away from the normal wind direction. Open the windows on the other side of the house to let air in; the fans will suck hot air out and the open windows will pull cooler air into your home.

Sage Advice

Indoor air, on average, is 2 to 5 times more polluted than the outdoor air.
Source: EPA

Use high-efficiency furnace filters like 3M, not fiberglass filters.

A dirty furnace filter will not clean your indoor air and it may even contribute to the pollution. It will also interfere with the furnaces ability to run efficiently and it can damage the furnace itself. Change your filters whenever they look dirty, but at least once every 3 months. When it's time to change, choose a high-efficiency furnace filter like those available from 3M that will filter out 90% of the large airborne particles polluting your air.

Use energy efficient air purifiers, not ozone generating devices.

Avoid "ionic" air purifiers, which generate ozone. Far from cleaning the air, ozone pollutes it and is a threat to your health. Instead, choose an air purifier with a HEPA (High Efficiency Particulate Air) filter that can remove 99% of the particulate matter in your air. Make sure you choose the right size for your space and clean or replace the filters regularly according to the manufacturer's instructions.

Use baking soda, not Carpet Fresh.

Carpet cleaners are typically filled with toxins that can cause long-term health problems including cancer. For a safer and cheaper carpet cleaner, use baking soda. Vacuum the carpet to get the dirt up, then sprinkle the baking soda and let it sit overnight or while you're at work. Vacuum until you don't see any more baking soda.

Sage Advice

Over 17 million people in the U.S. suffer from asthma. Add to this the 44 million homes in the U.S. (45% of all homes) that have a very serious dust mite problem and you get a recipe for asthma triggers!

AIR FRESHENERS
Green it!

YOUNG LIVING®
DIFFUSER WITH ESSEN-
TIAL OILS

THE GOOD

When essential oils are diffused, they release molecules that increase oxygen in the air. The oils then easily enter the nose and bloodstream, enhancing the body's capacity to transport oxygen and nutrients into the cells.

THE GREEN

Alleviate tension, disperse odors, and generate an atmosphere of peace and harmony by diffusing essential oils, which are thought to have a positive effect on your sense of smell (known as your olfactory system), and your limbic system, which encompasses your memory, emotion and motivation.

THE CONVENIENT TRUTH

French chemist René-Maurice Gatte-fossé coined the term "aromatherapy" in the early 1920s. Look for them in organic.

Lisa's D.I.Y.

According to a study by NASA scientists, indoor plants can remove more than carbon dioxide from your house; they can also remove chemical vapors and toxic gases from your air. Spider plants are great at removing formaldehyde, English ivy is great in absorbing benzene, and the rubber plant is a great all-around plant. A plant for every 100 square feet is recommended for optimal cleaning.

Sage Advice

In homes where air fresheners are used every day, nearly a third more babies suffer from diarrhea and significantly more earaches compared to homes using them once a week or less, according to University of Bristol's Children of the 90s study. Of mothers who used air fresheners and aerosols, 16% reported depression, compared to 12.7% of those who rarely used them. Mothers who used fresheners daily suffered nearly 10% more headaches.

Skip it!
SYNTHETIC SCENTED AIR FRESHENER

THE UGLY

The ironic thing about air fresheners is they can contain numerous harmful chemicals. Their synthetic fragrances can cause watery eyes, hea-daches, skin and respiratory irritation, asthma, and allergic reactions.

THE INCONVENIENT TRUTH

Phthalates, which hold the fragrances in these products, can intensify asthma and are associated with reproductive problems. They could also contain VOCs like xylene, ketones, and aldehydesas, as well as known carcinogens benzene and formaldehyde.

CHAPTER 1

KERMIT'S VIEW:

IT'S NOT EASY BEING GREEN!

TOP 10 SHOPPING MYTHS REVEALED, GREENWASHING TACTICS, AND PRODUCT LABELS DEFINED

TOP 10 SHOPPING MYTHS REVEALED

MYTH #1: "FRAGRANCE FREE" IS FREE OF ADDED CHEMICALS.

The "fragrance free" label is not meaningful and may even be deceptive. "Fragrance free" is a general claim that implies that the product does not contain any fragrances. But according to the Food and Drug Administration (FDA), there is no standard definition that governs the use of the term "fragrance free." Moreover, products labeled "fragrance free" can still contain fragrances that are used to cover up the chemical smell of the other ingredients in the product.

MYTH #2: ALL AIR PURIFIERS CLEAN YOUR AIR.

While there are quality air purifiers on the market that do a great job of cleaning your air, it's important to note that all "ionic" air purifiers emit some ozone. According to the EPA, when inhaled, ozone can damage the lungs. Even relatively low amounts can cause chest pain, coughing, shortness of breath, and throat irritation. Ozone may also worsen chronic respiratory diseases such as asthma and compromise the body's ability to fight respiratory infection. When you're shopping for an air purifier, be wary of any vendor that suggests that these devices have been approved by the federal government for use in occupied spaces. *No* agency of the federal government has approved these devices for use in occupied spaces.

MYTH #3: "NATURAL" MEANS THE PRODUCT COMES FROM NATURE.

This claim is often used, but not independently verified. The claim is placed on the product by the manufacturer and can mean "natural" in color. If a product is truly "natural," it should have a detailed ingredients list to back up the claim.

MYTH #4 "BIODEGRADABLE" IS GOOD FOR THE PLANET.

Everything is biodegradable *at some point*. Plastic bottles can take up to 500 years; diapers, up to 1,000 years. Just because a product or ingredient is biodegradable does not mean it is healthy and safe for you or the environment. For example, DDT biodegrades to the compounds DDD and DDE, both of which are more toxic and more dangerous than the original DDT.

MYTH #5: "ZERO VOC" PAINT DOES NOT CONTAIN CHEMICALS.

Volatile Organic Compounds (VOCs) pollute the air and have been linked to respiratory and memory problems. As more and more paint companies expand their "green" offerings, "Zero VOC" paint is becoming more widely available. However, it's important to know that "zero" is not exactly right. Federal VOC limits are now set at 250 grams per liter (g/l) for flat paints and 380 g/l for nonflats. Some states have been progressive on this issue and lowered the allowable VOC levels for paints. For example, California's standards are now 50 g/l for non-flat finishes and 100 g/l for flat. The EPA hopes to propose new, lower federal VOC regulations for a 2010 effective target. Finally, remember, your nose doesn't always know best. "Low Odor" paint and "Low VOC" paint are not created equal since odors from off-gassed VOC fumes may use chemicals to mask the smell. And even these greener paints can still contain toxic ingredients such as toluene, ammonia, phthalates, heavy metals, and glycol esters.

It's still a good idea to choose paints and finishes labeled low or no VOCs, but all the usual precautions while painting should be taken. Make sure your space is well ventilated, and do the painting when kids and pregnant women are not in the house.

MYTH #6: CANDLES WITH ESSENTIAL OILS USE ONLY NATURAL SCENTS.

Some candle products that claim to be scented with essential oils may contain as little as one drop of oil, which could be diluted with other synthetic fragrances. Candle manufacturers are not required by law to list their ingredients, so you have no way of knowing what you're actually breathing when you light your candle. In fact, the word "fragrance" or "parfum" in the ingredients list often masks *hundreds* of hidden chemicals. Even if a regular paraffin candle is scented with essential oils, it's still a petroleum-based candle that pollutes your air as it burns. Look for beeswax or soy candles that are unscented or that use 100% essential oils.

MYTH #7: PRODUCTS LABELED "ORGANIC" DO NOT CONTAIN TOXINS.

Many products use the word "organic" on their packaging. But unless the label is verified by a certifier or another independent inspection organization (e.g.: USDA), the term is not a reliable indicator of a safe and green product. That's because there is no way to guarantee that it was cultivated without pesticides or doesn't contain harmful chemicals. In fact, according to current guidelines, the word "organic" can appear on personal care products in which just one ingredient on the whole list is organic. Recently, some "organic" personal care products were found by the Organic Consumers Association to contain 1,4-Dioxane, which is a known carcinogen.

MYTH #8:
GOING GREEN WILL
COST YOU "GREEN."

With new "green" products hitting the market every day, it's easy to think it would cost you a fortune to truly go green. The truth is, going green isn't about buying all new furniture, cork flooring, and organic towels—although those are nice. It's really about the simple decisions you make every day and changing habits to conserve energy and reduce consumption.

Green Nest (www.GreenNest.com) offers a video and articles on how to go green for less than $250.00.

MYTH #9: AIR FRESHENERS
CLEAN THE AIR.

There are four basic ingredients in air fresheners: formaldehyde, petroleum distillates, p-dichlorobenzene, and aerosol propellants. In fact, air fresheners are created with any of over 3,000 synthetic chemical ingredients. Manufacturers are not required to list ingredients on the label, using instead the generic term "fragrance." Spraying toxins in the air is hardly anyone's idea of "freshening" it. In fact, many of these chemicals are not targeting the air but your nose's ability to smell. Others simply mask an existing smell with another.

MYTH #10: ALL INGREDIENTS ARE LISTED ON THE LABELS OF CLEANING, PERSONAL CARE, AND PESTICIDE PRODUCTS.

Since manufacturers are allowed to consider fragrance a "trade secret," the government does not require them to list the specific ingredients in a fragrance. As a result, consumers may not be able to identify the specific agent causing an allergic reaction from a product. Look for products that list and even explain all of their ingredients in clear view on their labels.

GREENWASHING

THE GREENWASHING INDEX IS AN online rating tool that exposes greenwashing practices. Greenwashing occurs when companies and organizations spend time and money claiming to be "green" through advertising and marketing, but do not actually back up their claim with equivalent environmental efforts. Their products may sound or appear to be healing the environment, but they are ultimately taking advantage of consumers. Source: www. greenwashingindex.com.

THE MANY SHADES OF GREENWASHING

According to the green marketing firm Terra-Choice, there are six primary ways that companies commit greenwashing.

1. Singular focus
Some companies make green claims by emphasizing one attribute of the product and ignoring everything else. For example, a sheet set may be labeled "eco-friendly" because it contains some bamboo in it, which is a renewable resource. Yet the sheet may also contain pesticide-intensive non-organic cotton. It may be colored with toxic dyes and treated with formaldehyde and other chemicals to prevent wrinkling, bacteria, and fire. The sheet may have been produced in China and transported to the United States using mega-amounts of fossil fuels. It may also be wrapped in PVC vinyl packaging, which contains toxins that are known to damage the hormonal system and cause cancer. Because PVC leaches heavy metals in the landfill and emits dangerous chemicals if incinerated, it is best treated as hazardous waste. Obviously, a little bamboo does not make a truly green product.

2. Claims with no proof
Walk up and down any supermarket aisle and you can see this in action. Claims are everywhere, but pick up the bottle or box and you'll

be hard pressed to find a certification or any other supporting evidence. Often, you won't be able to find the evidence on the product's website either.

3. Claims with no meaning

Claims like "All Natural" and "Green" are simply too broad to be clearly defined. Yet they continue to appear on product label after product label. Look beyond the claims at the packaging and ingredients list to evaluate the product.

4. Irrelevance

Claims may be truthful, but completely irrelevant to the person making a buying decision. For example, an air freshener may boast that it does not contain a toxic substance like chlorofluorocarbons (CFCs). Sounds great, but CFCs were banned in all products decades ago. Candles that promote "lead free wicks" are also guilty of this type of greenwashing. Lead is already banned from all wicks manufactured in the U.S., so the claim is irrelevant.

5. Distracting from the bigger picture

Some industries are simply not green no matter which way you look at them. However, companies within those industries continually try to get us to focus on one small green gesture like an investment in alternative energy or the use of some recycled materials in their packaging. By focusing our attention on what's green, however small, they hope that we forget much bigger environmental sins for which the company or industry is responsible. For example, the fact that a pack of cigarettes comes in recycled packaging does not make them "green."

6. Not-so-little green lies

Because there is no central regulatory body for all things "green," companies are still getting away with making completely false claims on their products. They may say a product is certified organic when no such certification was bestowed. Or they may state that the packaging comes from recycled materials, when it doesn't. It's important not to purchase products from companies who use this greenwashing tactic.

GREENWASHING IN ADVERTISING

Greenwashing in advertising can range from the very subtle to the outrageously obvious. The Greenwashing Index (www.greenwashingindex.com) recommends the following step-by-step formula for recognizing when advertisers are trying to throw the green wool over your eyes.

1. Focus on the words.

Some ads boldly state their false claims. Others use vague language such as "sustainable," "environmentally friendly," or "natural" to get you to think they are greener than they are.

2. Evaluate the images.

Does the label or ad contain images of a pristine forest or lake or an animal in the wild? Are there flowers and happy children? How do those images relate to the bigger picture of the environmental impact of this product or industry? Shell Oil uses images to greenwash in one of their UK ads. Pretty flowers, rather than toxic pollution spewing from refinery stacks, misrepresents and distracts from the true environmental toll of its business practices and industry.

3. Look for evidence.

If an ad or product label makes a claim, look for proof. Some claims like "natural" are simply too vague to ever be proven. Be suspicious. You can often find the evidence that disproves the claim right next to the claim on the label!

4. Don't let the 25% recycled packaging fool you.

Ortho's EcoSense is anything but "Eco." How do we know? The green claims share the label with a list of warnings that make it clear that this product is not just bad for the bugs. It's bad for the environment and your health. It is not safe to spray this product near any water, including storm drains or drainage ditches, or before it rains. It should not be sprayed when it's windy. And, if you get it on your skin, call poison control or your doctor immediately. The other tip-off? Less than a quarter of this product's ingredients are actually listed on the label.

5. Don't believe the hype.

The old adage that "if it looks too good to be true, it is" applies here. If the claims are so big and bold you find them hard to believe, you're probably right.

6. Consider what the ad isn't saying.

While one aspect of the product may be as green as the ad says, consider the larger picture: What resources went into the production of the product? What impact do they have on the environment? How far does the product travel for you to buy it? What's the environmental impact of the industry as a whole?

Monsanto is the producer of such unsustainable and un-green products as Round-up weed killer, Bovine Growth Hormone (rBGH) and, further back in history, Agent Orange. The EPA has pegged Monsanto as the likely culprit for 56 Superfund sites according to a 2002 confidential list obtained by the Center for Public Integrity. A Superfund site is a toxic waste site that falls under the Environmental Protection Agency's Superfund program. Monsanto is also the leader in producing genetically engineered seeds. It even developed a type of seed that is engineered to produce plants with sterile seeds. That means the farmer has no choice but to buy new seeds each year. Sustainable agriculture? Monsanto is reaching here as it puts up a nice green face to cover a whole history of environmental degradation.

7. Do some digging.

The Internet makes identifying greenwashing easier than ever. Watchdog groups like Greenwashing Index (www.greenwashingindex .com) and CorpWatch (www.corpwatch.org) are dedicated to identifying offenders and helping us sort the green from the greenwashed. When a company crosses the line consistently and outrageously, you may even find organizations and websites determined to educate consumers to see through the greenwashing. One example www.truecostof chevron.com—takes the oil giant's own feel-good and green "Human Energy" ad campaign and turns it on its head. The organization puts out an "Alternative Annual Report" that details all the environmental and human abuses. You can read it for yourself on their website.

Sage Advice

Lake Superior State University's "2009 List of Banished Words" included "green," "going green," "carbon footprint," and "carbon offsetting." The grounds for banishment? "mis-use, over-use and general uselessness." Source:http://www.lssu.edu/banished /current.php

GREEN FACTS

Healthy Rx
Take back our water's health by engaging in pharmaceutical take back programs. These offer locations for the public to bring unused drugs to a central location for proper disposal. Many pharmacies also offer this solution.

Sage Advice
EWG's reviewed 1,572 products of sunscreen and discovered 3 out of 5 sunscreens lack adequate protection from the sun or contain ingredients with major safety concerns. Check out their handy guide: www.ewg.org/files/2009sunscreenguide.pdf.

Sage Advice
You should only use reputable carbon offset companies. They provide tools to assist you in calculating your personal, family or business carbon footprint and the means to off-set those behavioral effects on global warming.

Sage Advice
The airline industry discarded 9,000 tons of plastic in 2004, according to The Natural Resources Defense Council. If you forgot to bring a reusable bottle on your next flight, try to go green. Look for canned, glass or boxed juices and make sure to recycle the containers later.

PRODUCT LABELS

Green it!

LEAPING BUNNY-CERTIFIED LABEL / USDA CERTIFIED ORGANIC LABEL

THE GOOD

The Leaping Bunny Program administers a cruelty-free standard for companies producing cosmetic, personal care, and household products, assuring that no new animal testing is used in any particular phase of product development by the company, its laboratories, or suppliers. Take the pledge at: www.leapingbunny/pledge.

THE GREEN

The USDA Label (U.S. Department of Agriculture) created standards that must be met by anyone using the "organic" label in the U.S. The National Organic Program (NOP)'s USDA label certification for products, aids consumers in their purchasing decision of organic cotton fabrics, dairy, fruit and vegetable and livestock and organic body care items.

Sage Advice

Here's a USDA labeling guide. Goods labeled **Made with Organic Ingredients** must be made with at least 70% organic ingredients.
USDA Organic must consist of at least 95% organically produced ingredients.
USDA 100% Organic must contain only organic ingredients.

Skip it!
WARNING, CAUTION, OR DANGER LABELS

THE UGLY

The Consumer Product Safety Commission (CSPC) regulates the labeling of hazardous household cleaning products but does not test or certify products. They rely on the companies and manufacturers themselves to provide testing on safety.

THE INCONVENIENT TRUTH

Defined by the CPSC, the warning labels "Danger" and "Poison" indicate that a product is corrosive, flammable or combustible, irritating, or a strong sensitizer, and that they have the potential to cause serious personal injury or illness during, or as a result of, normal use. Specific labels are required depending on the level and type of toxicity and include Danger, Caution, Warning, Flammable, Harmful if Swallowed, Causes Burns, and Poison.

Sage Advice

As part of the USDA organic standard requirement, most synthetic and petroleum derived pesticides and fertilizers are prohibited for use in organic production. For more information visit www.ams.usda.gov.

COMMON GREEN TERMS

Don't assume that environmental and health claims are true. In many cases, manufacturers can make claims that are neither independently verified nor regulated. Here's a selection of some of the most common claims you'll find on green and greenwashed products alike:

Nontoxic

The term suggests that the product is not dangerous to our health or planet. But the claim is often used on products that are not independently verified. So it's just the manufacturer making the claim on the label. Unless there is a third party certification to stand behind and define the term, it's not a claim you can trust.

Natural or All Natural

If you see these terms on labels, keep reading. The term is not defined or regulated so anyone can use it. Also keep in mind that there are plenty of "natural" substances like arsenic that are not necessarily safe or good for you.

Green, Environmentally Friendly, Eco Friendly, and Eco-Conscious

All four claims are meaningless unless they share the label with some proof. Look for reputable third party certifications such as Green Seal or USDA Organic. There should also be a full and complete ingredients list. Evaluate the packaging. Is it made from recycled material and recyclable? For a product to make these claims, it should walk the walk.

Biodegradable

This term suggests that the item and its packaging will decompose in a short period of time. However the term is not regulated enough to make it meaningful. Since practically everything will biodegrade given enough time and/or a nice sunny field or compost heap, the claim can easily be made without necessarily lying.

Chemical free

This claim is always false because there is nothing on the planet that is actually free of chemicals. Water, air, minerals are all made up of chemical components. If you see this claim on a label, don't buy it.

Hypoallergenic

With no regulation for this term, it's hardly a good indicator of whether the product will be safe.

Sustainable

The United Nations defines the term *sustainable* as follows: "To meet the needs of the present without compromising the ability of future generations to meet their own needs." It is often used to describe farming or forest management practices that do not harm the environment. Like most of these terms, it is used too often and taken too lightly to be truly meaningful on a label. It's better to look for certifications to back it up. For example, wood that has been certified by the Forest Stewardship Council (FSC) comes from forests that are well managed for the good of the environment and the local people.

Carbon Neutral

This does not mean that the production of the product did not create carbon, but that the company "offset" the carbon it did produce by investing in renewable energy. This is a good step, but keep the big picture in view. Carbon neutral bottled water still has all the environmental and health concerns of regular old bottled water. Carbon offset programs are yet unregulated and not all are created equally.

CHAPTER 2

GOING GREEN CAN SAVE YOU GREEN

TIPS & IDEAS TO REDUCE DAILY EXPENSES

TOP 10 MONEY SAVING IDEAS

1. USE YOUR OWN CLEANERS, NOT STORE BROUGHT.

Instead of throwing out your conventional cleaners and springing for all new green cleaners, try making your own with some ingredients you may already have on hand. It's a great idea to finish the cleaners you have and re-use the spray bottles and other containers to make your green cleaners. Then you can buy just a few essential ingredients in bulk and reduce the amount of packaging you contribute to the waste stream.

Vinegar, not Windex

Mix 2 cups water and 1 cup white distilled vinegar in a spray bottle. If you've been using a conventional cleaner like Windex, you'll need to add a few drops of dish soap to help get rid of the film the cleaner leaves behind. After cleaning with this mixture a few times, the film will be gone and you can just use water and vinegar. Instead of paper towels, use newspaper to clean the glass. It won't leave bits of paper on the glass and it cleans great. You may want to wear gloves to protect your hands from the newsprint.

Essential oils, not Glade Plug-Ins

Conventional air fresheners do nothing to actually freshen the air. Instead, they either interfere with our sense of smell or mask whatever odor you have with another odor, simultaneously creating a nightmare for those with allergies or asthma. Use essential oil scented candles or a diffuser to scent your home. Or mix 10 drops of your favorite oil with 2 cups of water in a small spray bottle. Choose lavender to promote sleep and rosemary to wake you up.

Toothpaste, not silver polish

Silver polishes contain toxins that can easily be avoided by using toothpaste. Choose a no-frills toothpaste without baking soda or coloring so you don't scratch your silver. Just scrub, rinse and dry. For heirloom silver, use the polishing cloths that came with the silver. Remember that the more you use your silver, the less tarnish you'll have!

Olive oil, not Pledge

Conventional furniture polish contains ingredients that are neurotoxic and carcinogenic. Who wants to eat off of a table polished with dangerous toxins? Switch from conventional polishes to a do-it-yourself polish of ½-cup distilled white vinegar to 1-teaspoon olive oil.

Wool dryer balls, not Bounce

Dryer sheets are often heavy on the fragrance, which means they don't have to list any number of known toxins on their label. Wool dryer balls, not to be confused with plastic dryer balls, not only soften your fabric, but they can reduce your drying time because they separate the clothes as they circulate.

ALL-PURPOSE CLEANERS

Green it!

BON AMI® / BAKING SODA / GREEN WORKS® DISH SOAP

THE GOOD
Bon Ami has been around for over 120 years and contains no dyes, phosphorus, chlorine or fragrance.

- -

THE GREEN
Bon Ami is nontoxic and biodegradable; great for those with allergies or chemical sensitivities. It prevents the formation of mold and mildew which can be sources of indoor pollution.

- -

THE CONVENIENT TRUTH
Bon Ami's oxygen bleach brightens with no toxic fumes and the powdered soap cuts straight through greasy grime.

- -

Ron's Green $$ Tip
Make your own soft scrub! Mix baking soda and natural/biodegradable dish soap. Stir until it forms a paste. That's it—healthy and economical.

Skip it!

BLEACH-CONTAINING SCRUB

THE UGLY

Have you ever gotten a cleaner on your skin or clothing? According to one major brand's MSDS (Material Safety Data Sheet): "INHALATION: Not a likely route of exposure. Irritating, in high concentration, to the respiratory tract (nose, throat, and lungs). SKIN CONTACT: Can cause mild skin irritation with prolonged contact . . ." HANDLING: "Do not get in eyes, on skin, on clothing. Do not take internally. Use with adequate ventilation. . . ."

THE INCONVENIENT TRUTH

The average person breathes 10 to 20 thousand liters of air per day. Chemicals can be absorbed through the skin or through inhalation or ingestion.

Sage Advice

Nature's Source Natural Bathroom Cleaner by SC Johnson is made with plant-based surfactants derived from natural substances such as coconut oil or palm-kernel oil to remove dirt, soil, and grime. It also uses lactic acid which is produced from fruits, vegetables, and a variety of other sources to remove hard-water deposits. All of this combined with purified H_2O makes for one healthy cleaner!

2. USE PLANTS FOR AIR PURIFICATION, NOT SO-CALLED IONIC-AIR PURIFIERS.

When you consider that you breathe in 10 to 20 thousand liters of air every day, you can see how important it is to make sure it's clean. As stated previously, ionic air purifiers emit ozone, which pollutes your air even as it works to clean it. Luckily, there are certain widely available houseplants that can do a great job of cleaning your air. (See below.) In fact, one potted plant per 100 square feet will clean the air in an average home.

The TOP 10 plants most effective in removing formaldehyde, benzene, and carbon monoxide from the air include:

1. Bamboo Palm
2. Chinese Evergreen
3. English Ivy, Gerber Daisy
4. Janet Craig
5. Marginata
6. Corn Plant
7. Mother-In-Law's Tongue
8. Pot Mum
9. Peace Lily
10. Warnekii

3. USE HIGH-EFFICIENCY PLEATED FILTERS, NOT FIBERGLASS FILTERS.

Your heating and cooling filter may be your main defense against indoor air pollution. But keep in mind that it needs changing at least every 3 months. If you don't, it means the dirt, dander, and pollen collect and the filter can't clean anymore. High efficiency pleated filters are more effective because they have more surface area for the air to pass through. A cleaner air filter will help increase efficiency and can equal savings on your heating and cooling bills.

4. USE ENERGY STAR APPLIANCES, NOT OLDER MODELS.

It may seem cheaper and even greener to just to stick with your older refrigerator or dishwasher. But consider how much money you're paying in energy bills and how much energy you're wasting with your old machines. Switching to appliances rated Energy Star by the U.S. Department of Energy means you'll save about $75 each year in energy bills, and you'll use 10% to 50% less energy and water.

5. USE A HOME WATER FILTRA-TION SYSTEM, NOT TAP WATER.

While your local government water agency may deem your tap water safe, the list of contaminants they test for is surprisingly short. A home water filtration system will help ensure that the water you're drinking and showering in is safe and healthy for everyone in your family.

6. USE STAINLESS-STEEL CONTAIN-ERS, NOT PLASTIC BOTTLES.

When you consider that only 20% of recyclable bottles ever make it to the recycler, you can see the scope of the problem. Instead of buying bottled water, invest in a reusable stainless steel container. (See page 54.)

7. USE A COFFEE MUG, NOT PAPER CUPS.

Starbucks goes through 3 *billion* disposable paper cups a year. Why add one more? Buy a reusable cup and you'll not only save cups from going to the landfill, but you'll save some money on your coffee since Starbucks offers a $0.10 discount when you bring your own cup.

8. GO SOLAR, NOT ELECTRIC.

Once the badge of the green elite, solar is now in the realm of the possible for the rest of us. Innovation and tax credits mean that going solar has never been more affordable.

9. USE SURGE PROTECTORS, NOT WALL OUTLETS.

Surge protectors not only protect your electronics, but they also make it easy to turn all your machines off at the end of the day. Some surge protectors are so smart they can actually turn off your equipment when they sense you are no longer using it! That way you can conserve energy even when you forget to turn them off yourself.

10. TURN THE CAR OFF, DON'T IDLE AND WASTE GAS.

If traffic is at a standstill for longer than a minute, turn your car off. Restart it when you're ready to go. This can actually save up to 19% of the gas you use.

CONTAINERS

Green it!

KLEAN KANTEEN® / THINK SPORT / THERMOS STAINLESS STEEL INTAK® HYDRATION BOTTLE

THE GOOD
United Nations members estimate it would only take half of the $100 billion spent annually on bottled water to invest in the needed water infrastructure and treatment for everyone in the world to have access to clean drinking water.

- -

THE GREEN
NRDC studies revealed 40% of bottled water is indeed just tap water. The EPA sets *stricter quality standards for tap water* than the FDA does for bottled drinks.

- -

THE CONVENIENT TRUTH
Reduce the huge amount of plastic bottles produced for bottled water by investing in a reusable stainless steel container. They come in a variety of sizes and you can take them everywhere you go.

- -

Healthy Rx

Avoid choosing products that use polyvinyl chloride (#3), polystyrene (#6), and polycarbonate (#7). In addition, PET (#1) products are only intended for single use and should not be reused.

Note: If you purchased a SIGG aluminum bottle prior to August 2008, you can return it for a full refund because 2009 testing has revealed the bottle liners did contain Bisphenol-A contrary to SIGG's inference that they did not contain BPA.

Skip it!
HARMFUL PLASTICS

THE UGLY
Over time, plastic bottles that made from PET (#1) can wear and break down, releasing the chemical DEHA (a known carcinogen) into the liquid.

THE INCONVENIENT TRUTH
Beverage container waste has increased more than 50% from 1992 to 1999, going from 63.4 billion containers to 96.9 billion.

CHAPTER 3

YOUR WORLD:

EASY WAYS TO HELP MOTHER NATURE & AND PRESERVE PLANET EARTH

Use Nokia or Samsung, not Microsoft, HP, or Nintendo.

Shopping for greener electronics means going beyond simple comparisons of prices and features. It's important to also consider the manufacturer's record on the environment. Greenpeace's "Guide to Greener Electronics" ranks the bestselling electronics manufacturers based on their use of toxic chemicals, recycling, and global warming. Nokia tops the list because of its progressive "take-back" program that keeps its phones out of the landfills. Samsung is in second place because of its commitment to reduce its greenhouse gas emissions and its leading role in phasing out some of the worst toxins found in electronics.

Use online shopping or swap items, not the mall.

Shopping online uses about a third less energy than actually going to the mall or other retail stores to make your purchases. Plus, if you're buying gifts to send to family or friends, you'll use the energy it takes to go to the store plus the energy it takes to ship the gifts. When you buy online, those gifts can be shipped directly to the recipient. Amazingly, even if you ship your products via overnight air, you'll still use 40% less energy than you would driving around to shop. However, ground shipping is six times more fuel-efficient than air shipping so it is obviously the greener choice.

Use Shorebank Pacific or ING Direct, not a mega-bank.

The mega-bank industry continues to invest in projects that wreak havoc on the environment such as coal plants and mining operations. Since it's your money they're investing, choose a bank with values that match your own. Shorebank Pacific is one option. It invests in environmental conservation and economic development projects in the Pacific Northwest.

Another way to green your banking is to do it online instead of driving across town to your branch. You can put the gas money you save into an ING Direct savings account and earn higher interest than you would at most branch banks.

Sage Advice

Warehouses used for online retail businesses use only about $\frac{1}{16}$th of the energy it takes to run a brick and mortar store.

Another green option is to use www. freecycle.org to find items that are in good condition without having to buy them new. This is also a great way to declutter your home without filling up the landfill!

Use a Working Assets credit card, not Bank of America and Citigroup.

When Green America ranked the mega-banks on their environmental and human rights records, not one of them scored above a C. Bank of America and Citigroup were at the very bottom of an already poor-performing heap. The poor rankings for some of the banks are based on financing projects, including coal-powered energy plants and mining in the Amazon River basin that cause harm to the environment. Additionally, avoid companies whose unsustainable investments from the banking industry even used proceeds to fund the forces that carry out the genocide in Darfur.

At the opposite end of the spectrum, Working Assets' mission is to support the environment and human rights, and they've donated millions to these causes. Every time you use their credit card, Working Assets donates 10 cents to charities that include the Wilderness Society, Natural Resources Defense Council, and Rainforest Action Network.

Use Credo Mobile vs. Sprint, AT&T, and Verizon.

You pay your cell phone bill every month anyway, why not have a portion of the money go to help protect the environment? Credo Mobile (www.credomobile.com), which is part of Working Assets, donates 1% of all charges to progressive organizations such as Greenpeace, and says they have donated more than $10 million to environmental groups.

Use Better World Mortgage to find a mortgage broker, not the yellow pages.

As more comes to light about the shady practices used by some of the big mortgage lenders, it's nice to know that some in the industry are still trying to do good. Better World Mortgage connects homebuyers and owners with environmentally and socially conscious mortgage brokers in their area. Those brokers then donate 10% of their gross income to the charity you choose. The best part? Their donation is in your name so you get the tax write off!

Use Healthy Alternatives, not Conventional Dry Cleaning

Conventional dry cleaners use perchlorethylene, or perc, to clean your clothes. Perc is a Volatile Organic Compound and a strongly suspected carcinogen and air pollutant. This is bad for workers and people who live above or near dry cleaners. But perc is still present in your clothes when you bring them home and hang them in your closet. Leaving them in the plastic bag means the toxin will stick around longer and you'll breathe it in every time you go into your closet. Try these alternatives:

HAND WASH Many garments that are labeled "Dry Clean Only" actually come out great when you wash them by hand. Just fill a sink with cool water, use a mild dishwashing soap, and soak them for 10 minutes. Gently press out the water. Place on a towel to dry.

LEARN TO IRON Much of what gets taken to the dry cleaner is more wrinkled than dirty. With the right iron and some technique, it's easy to iron quickly and effectively. For best results, look for irons that give off tons of steam. They will cut your ironing time down dramatically.

PROFESSIONAL WET CLEANING

Wet cleaners use computer-controlled equipment and mild, biodegradable detergents. It's safe for most fabrics and, in recent tests by Consumer Reports, wet cleaning performed better than traditional dry cleaning.

LIQUID CARBON DIOXIDE CLEANING (CO_2 CLEANING)

This cleaning process takes the CO_2 that is the byproduct of other industrial production and "recycles" it into the primary solvent to clean your clothes.

Don't use these types of Dry Cleaning

LIQUID CARBON DIOXIDE CLEANING—SOLVAIR METHOD

This method is similar to CO_2 cleaning, but it only uses the recycled CO_2 in the finishing process. The primary solvent used to clean garments is actually glycol ether, which is linked to neurological, respiratory, cardiovascular and kidney problems.

"GREENEARTH®" CLEANING

Despite the eco name, this type of cleaning is not actually green. It uses a silicone-based solvent that has been shown to cause cancer in rats.

HYDROCARBON DRY CLEANING

Hydrocarbon is derived from petroleum. Like conventional dry cleaning's toxic solvent, perc, hydrocarbon is a Volatile Organic Compound.

Use refillable cartridges, not new ones.

Globally, 1.1 billion printer cartridges go to landfills every year. Consider refilling the cartridges you already have. You'll save about half the cost of a new cartridge and be doing right by the planet. OfficeMax, Walgreens, and CartridgeWorld all have refill stations in their stores.

BATTERIES
Green it!

RECHARGEABLE BATTERIES

THE GOOD
Some battery chargers can take less than two hours to charge a battery. Original NiCd batteries used to take as long as 24 hours to recharge.

THE GREEN
Rechargeable batteries will save you money and help reduce waste compared to single use versions.

THE CONVENIENT TRUTH
Although disposable batteries are less toxic than rechargeable batteries, many more end up in our landfills. Additionally, rechargeable batteries are recycled more often and have a much longer lifecycle.

Ron's Green $$ Tip
It takes only a few times of recycling batteries for them to pay for themselves. Rechargeable batteries like the Duracell NiMH batteries can be charged hundreds of times without losing the ability to hold a charge.

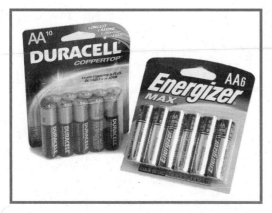

Sage Advice

Americans purchase nearly 3 billion dry-cell batteries every year, according to the EPA. Many of these contain toxic heavy metals like cadmium, mercury, and lead. Cadmium can cause damage to the kidneys, birth defects, and cancer. Mercury and lead are very potent neurotoxins. When batteries end up in the landfill, these toxins can contaminate water supplies. Using rechargeable batteries reduces the number of batteries going to the landfill. However, it's important to keep in mind that rechargeables also contain toxins and should be disposed of accordingly. Go to www.call2recycle.org for more information on recycling your batteries.

Skip it!

NON-RECHARGEABLE BATTERIES

THE UGLY

Unlike single-use batteries, toxic heavy metals such as cadmium, nickel and lead are contained in many rechargeable batteries. However, the long life of rechargeable batteries and myriad of recycling centers means these metals are more likely to be diverted from the waste stream.

THE INCONVENIENT TRUTH

Many terms used by battery manufactures can be misleading, and there are no industry standards. For example, the term "heavy duty" is frequently linked to the least powerful of batteries, and some "quick charger" batteries can take as long as seven hours to recharge! For more information on batteries go to www.greenbatteries.com.

After all,
you are as your land
and your air is.

—GERTRUDE STEIN

CHAPTER 4

YOUR HOME:

EVERY BREATH YOU TAKE, EVERY BED YOU MAKE, WE'LL BE GREENING YOU!

PEST CONTROL

Green it!

CAYENNE / CITRUS OIL / CINNAMON / BORAX POWDER EXTREME BUG VAC / AFM SAFECOAT CAULKING

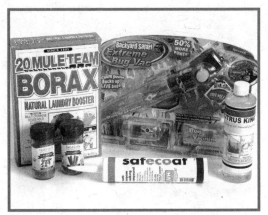

THE GOOD
It's easy to remove ants and other pests without having to resort to using toxic pesticide sprays and bait traps. Find great solutions at www.BeyondPesticides.org.

THE GREEN
Soapy water will not only kill individual ants, but it also removes the chemical trail that other lines of ants follow. Or try the Bug Vacuum, which helps support our ecosystem by relocating the insect instead of harming it.

THE CONVENIENT TRUTH
Ants follow chemical trails left by other ants to help them find food sources. Following this path backward can help you identify their point of entry in your home. You can eventually seal that part of your home with a less toxic caulking (e.g.: AFM Safecoat).

Sage Advice
Leave out a small piece of cardboard covered in a mixture of borax (bait) and syrup or a high protein treat (depending on type of ant) overnight. The ants will return the bait to the colony. Allow up to 10 days to complete the cycle and keep out of children's reach.

Skip it!
TOXIC PESTICIDES

THE UGLY
Research has shown higher rates of leukemia and brain cancer in children who live in homes where pesticides are used and a 3 to 7 times greater chance of developing Non-Hodgkin's Lymphoma for those living where insecticides and extermination methods are applied.

THE INCONVENIENT TRUTH
Be aware of so-called "inert" ingredients labeled on pesticides sprays and bait traps. Some of these inert ingredients have been shown to be *more toxic* than the active ingredients and even receive less testing.

Mother Knows Best!
Coffee grounds, lemon juice, cinnamon, cayenne pepper, and citrus oil are all natural remedies for creating a barrier of entry into your home from ants.

WEED KILLER

Green it!

VINEGAR / EMPTY SPRAY BOTTLE

THE GOOD
White vinegar is great at removing small weeds and is a healthier alternative to toxic herbicides.

- -

THE GREEN
Five million U.S. households use only all-natural / organic weed control, based on a 2004 national survey by the National Gardening Association and Organic Gardening Magazine.

- -

THE CONVENIENT TRUTH
Dogs exposed to herbicide-treated lawns and gardens have *double* the chance of developing canine lymphoma.

- -

Sage Advice
Fabric groundcovers are great at blocking out sunlight that can grow weeds on your lawn. Use with mulch for a great nontoxic solution. You can find them at local home improvement stores.

Skip it!

TOXIC HERBICIDES

THE UGLY
Of the thirty commonly used lawn pesticides, almost two-thirds of them are linked to carcinogenicity or cancer.

THE INCONVENIENT TRUTH
Manufacturers are not required to list inert ingredients on packaging; because of this, there is really no way to know what unidentified hazards may be present.

Research shows children under one year of age who have been exposed to herbicide have 4 times greater chance of getting asthma.

Sage Advice
Every year around 100 million pounds of Glyphosate, the active ingredient in Round Up are applied to American lawns and farms. Unfortunately, glyphosate is a pesticide that is linked to non-Hodgkin's lymphoma and even has acute human health effects. Research on Round Up has found that one of the "inert" ingredients amplifies its toxic effects on human cells. For more info, visit www.BeyondPesticides.org.

MATTRESSES

Green it!

NATURAL RUBBER & PURE WOOL MATTRESS

THE GOOD

One-third of your life is spent resting; maximize this time by laying on a healthy mattress! Select a certified organic mattress to avoid harmful chemicals like pesticides or flame-retardants.

THE GREEN

Natural fibers breathe better, and so will you. Look for pure virgin wool, certified organic cotton, natural latex rubber, or hemp to replace foams and synthetics.

THE CONVENIENT TRUTH

A temperature regulator, wool is naturally flame retardant and resistant to water and odor. The natural lanolin in wool also has the added benefit of repelling dust mites.

Lisa's D.I.Y.

To keep dust mites at bay, wash your bedding once a week in warm to hot water (at least 120 degrees). Or block the entry of dust mites by placing organic (not synthetic) "barrier cloth" covers over your mattress and pillows.

Skip it!
SYNTHETIC INNERSPRING MATTRESS

THE UGLY

What's in a mattress? For starters, it is stuffed with polyurethane foam (derived from petroleum) and treated with dangerous flame retardant chemicals. Cover that with fabric doused in water-, stain-, and wrinkle-resistant treatments. Add to these the chemicals emitted from polyurethane foam, such as toluene, and you have a recipe for indoor air pollution.

THE INCONVENIENT TRUTH

Mattress producers are not required to disclose the type of flame retardant chemicals used in the manufacturing process. Federal law only requires the label to state the adherence to the law.

Sage Advice

Don't throw away your mattress—donate or recycle it instead of letting the new mattress delivery-men just haul it away. Statistics reveal Americans throw away about 20 million mattresses each year. Check with www.Earth911.org to find a mattress recycler in your area.

PILLOWS
Green it!
NATURAL RUBBER PILLOW

THE GOOD
Natural latex rubber, wool, organic cotton, Kapok, and shredded or molded rubber with an organic cotton cover are all excellent materials to look for when choosing a pillow.

THE GREEN
Direct sunlight will kill dust mites while reducing moisture on bedding. Or, throw open the windows to provide a constant flow of fresh air. Use of barrier covers, vacuuming with a HEPA filter, or tossing your pillow in the dryer for 10 minutes help keep dust mites at bay.

THE CONVENIENT TRUTH
While we sleep, our bodies are far more sensitive to environmental influences and toxins than while awake.

Sage Advice
On average, seven times as many pounds of toxic fertilizer are regularly used on cotton crops than are pesticides. Cotton fertilizers and pesticides pollute the air, rivers, groundwater basins, and aquifers, in turn harming millions of fish and birds, not to mention thousands of rural inhabitants.

Skip it!

POLYURETHANE MEMORY FOAM PILLOW

THE UGLY

Synthetic pillows made from petroleum by-products do not have the ability to breath during warm weather like natural materials and fillings do.

THE INCONVENIENT TRUTH

Off-gassing (the passive release of chemicals after production) is typical with most polyurethane products such as memory foam. Instead, choose pillows like Kapok, derived from the seedpod of the kapok tree. It's a great alternative for those who prefer down—without the allergens.

Healthy Rx

Natural rubber or natural latex is made from the common rubber tree (Hevea brasiliensis.) Natural rubber contains an antibacterial substance that is a natural dust-mite repellent. It also absorbs moisture, inhibits the growth of mold or mildew, and regulates heat, all while providing optimal support.

BED SHEETS

Green it!

COYUCHI® ORGANIC SHEETS / HOME BAMBOO SHEETS

THE GOOD

Since skin is our largest organ, paying particular attention to what you sleep on one-third of your life can have a dramatic impact on your health and well being—choose organic products free of pesticides.

THE GREEN

The Coyuchi line has been recognized for its role in bolstering the production of organic cotton. It received the United Nations Second Annual Fashion Industry Award for Environmental Excellence.

THE CONVENIENT TRUTH

Bamboo sheets are supremely soft jersey knit sheets made from a renewable resource. Bamboo is a sustainable choice and comfortable.

Sage Advice

The highly-subsidized cotton industry consumes over 25% of all insecticides and 12% of all pesticides in the world, making it the most contaminated crop.

Skip it!
NONORGANIC WRINKLE-FREE SHEETS

THE UGLY
Avoid labels that read "wrinkle free," "no iron," or "easy care." Most are poly-cotton blends and are treated with a formaldehyde resin to keep the fabric from wrinkling. Research shows that cotton/polyester blend fabrics burn much quicker than 100% cotton.

THE INCONVENIENT TRUTH
Natural or cotton sheets are not the same as organic. Only *certified organic fabrics* can guarantee the removal of pesticides and other harmful chemicals.

Healthy Rx
Organic sheets are available in every price point and style. The Coyuchi Organic sheets are made with luxurious 100% certified organic cotton and come in a variety of styles like percale and damask. Check out other high-end brands like Ralph Lauren's first organic-cotton bedding collection and Anna Sova's luxury silk line. No need to compromise style or health.

PILLOW BARRIER COVERS

Green it!

ORGANIC COTTON PILLOW COVER

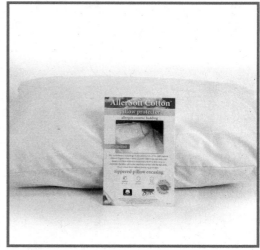

THE GOOD

"An unmade bed each morning may actually help keep you healthy," according to researchers at Kingston University in the UK because the linens on an unmade bed retain less moisture, making it less attractive to dust mites.

THE GREEN

Look for organic barrier covers made with SKAL (an inspection body for organic textile production, which verifies conformity with the organic regulations of Europe, Japan, and the U.S.) certified organic cotton that contains zero chemicals or urethanes. Prevent dust mites from entering and laying their eggs in your pillow by choosing barrier covers made with a high thread count and heat-pressed fabric to tighten the fibers, along with tight teeth on the zipper, keeping the goonies at bay!

THE CONVENIENT TRUTH

Your body sheds millions of dead skin flakes and you perspire 75 ml of fluid while snoozing. Could be why estimates from Ohio State University claims 10% of the weight of a two-year-old pillow can be composed of dead mites and their droppings.

Skip it!

NONORGANIC ALLERGY PILLOW COVER

THE UGLY

What thrives in warm, moist conditions and is so small several of them will fit on the end of a pin? They lurk in your mattress, pillow, and bedding, feeding on dead skin cells and excreted body fluids as you sleep. Commonly known as dust mites, they are miniature relatives of ticks and spiders.

THE INCONVENIENT TRUTH

The stuffing in pillows and comforters, even so-called natural fillers such as feathers, can actually harbor dust mites who need shed skin, moisture, and warmth to survive. Dust mites leave microscopic droppings, which, when inhaled, cause allergic reactions in many people.

Healthy Rx

Avoid barrier covers made with synthetic materials. Some allergy and moisture encasement are made of a microdenier fabric with fluid resistant finish, and the anti-microbial, Microban, is added to the fabric. Opt for a tighly woven cover made of 100% organic fabric like the Allersoft protector instead.

CARPET

Green it!

EARTH WEAVE®'S BIO-FLOR / FLOR™ / MOHAWK® SMARTSTRAND®

THE GOOD
Mohawk's EverStrand carpeting contains 100% post-consumer recycled content.

THE GREEN
One in every four plastic bottles recycled in North America becomes luxuriously soft Mohawk carpet. They recycle over 3 billion plastic bottles each year.

THE CONVENIENT TRUTH
You can fill a 10 gallon tank of gas with how much energy is saved making 70 yards of Mohawk's SmartStrand with DuPont Sorona.

Sage Advice
Earth Weave's Bio-Floor is great for both the environment and those suffering from chemical sensitivity. This 100% nontoxic and all natural carpet uses pure wool with no dyes, pesticides, or stain guards and a backing made of hemp fibers and jute. Even the nontoxic, biodegradable adhesive is derived from the rubber tree!

Skip it!

SYNTHETIC CARPETING WITH TOPICAL TREATMENTS

THE UGLY

Carpet is a haven for dust, dirt, mold and bacteria. Many types of carpeting also contain harmful chemicals and off-gas VOCs. Avoid purchasing synthetic carpeting, instead chose options like wool, sea grass, jute, and other natural fibers.

THE INCONVENIENT TRUTH

Many carpets are chemically treated with Teflon stain resistance, and wool carpets are often sprayed with moth-proofing pesticides, all of which emit toxic gases. Look for carpet that comes with a nontoxic backing and uses either nontoxic adhesives or tack-down installation.

Mother Knows Best!

Give your carpet back—through FLOR's Return & and Recycle program. They turn your old FLOR carpet squares into new product, most of which meet or exceed the Carpet and Rug Institute's (CRI) Green Label Plus standards for low VOCs. Low VOCs is key because of the impact on indoor air quality.

FLOORING
Green it!

MARMOLEUM FLOORING

THE GOOD
It's easy to find eco-friendly options for flooring. Great examples are bamboo flooring, FSC wood flooring (Eco-Timber), or reclaimed hardwood (Mohawk), tile, cork, Marmoleum, or concrete flooring. Mohawk's line of reclaimed hardwood flooring includes materials from ancient buildings that are over 600 years old!

THE GREEN
Produced with natural raw materials, Marmoleum has no undesirable health issues during any of the stages—beginning with its manufacturing, through its useful life, and up until its disposal. Installed with solvent free adhesives it doesn't allow for harmful VOCs to be emitted.

THE CONVENIENT TRUTH
Install hard surfaces in bathrooms, laundry rooms, kitchens or other moist areas where mold can easily grow.

Lisa's D.I.Y.
When purchasing wood flooring, always look for The Forest Stewardship Council (FSC)-Certified wood, which guarantees that the wood comes from a certified well-managed forest.

Skip it!

VINYL FLOORING

THE UGLY

Phthalates (pronounced tha-lates) can be found in PVC product such as vinyl flooring and are released into the air as they break down. Due to the sources found inside, air levels are on average much higher than outside.

THE INCONVENIENT TRUTH

Higher levels of airborne phthalates can be caused by raised air temperatures.

Sage Advice

Two types of phthalates, BBP and DEHP, which are prevalently in dust, are found in higher concentrations due to PVC flooring.

INSULATION
Green it!
BONDED LOGIC® ULTRATOUCH INSULATION

THE GOOD
Healthy alternative insulation materials include wool, cotton, or cellulose.

THE GREEN
Go for insulation made from blue jeans—Bonded Logic's UltraTouch—a brand of organic, eco-friendly, 100% recycled denim insulation.

THE CONVENIENT TRUTH
Second Nature, located in northern England, produces Thermafleece, which incorporates a patented sheep's wool building insulation.

Sage Advice
Spray-in foam starts out in liquid form, but expands and solidifies almost instantly to fill tiny cracks. It is highly flexible and allows trapped moisture to evaporate. Warning: some of these formulas are chemical minefields, while others, such as Icynene, are water blown and produce no off-gassing.

Sage Advice

Cellulose is an economical and effective alternative to fiberglass and is simple to install. It's also eco-friendly, since it is essentially recycled newspaper shredded to bits and sprayed into a space. However, be aware that shredded newspaper is highly combustible, pests like it, and water loves it, allowing it to get moldy.

Skip it!

FIBERGLASS INSULATION

THE UGLY

Although the evidence is unclear, many groups claim the health issues caused by fiberglass are just as bad as asbestos. The tiny sharp particles of fiberglass can break away into the air and embed in your skin, eyes, and lungs, creating small abrasions that cause irritation.

THE INCONVENIENT TRUTH

Formaldehyde, a cancer-causing chemical, can be released in potentially dangerous levels by fiberglass batting insulation.

FURNACE FILTERS

Green it!

HIGH PERFORMANCE 3M FILTRETE™ FILTERS

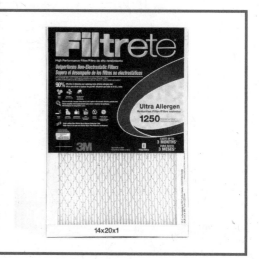

THE GOOD
Use a high efficiency furnace filter to decrease airborne allergens in your home, such as the Filtrete micro particle and airborne allergen reduction filter from 3M.

THE GREEN
You breathe 20,000 breaths and 3,400 gallons of air, on average, each day. A high efficiency filter, like the Filtrete brand, removes large airborne allergens throughout the home including mold, pollen and dust mites as well as microscopic particles such as smoke, smog and pet dander.

THE CONVENIENT TRUTH
Fifty percent of Americans are breathing air dirty enough to endanger lives! Want to know how your city stacks up? Check out the State the Air report compliments of the American Lung Association at: www.StateOfTheAir.org.

Lisa's D.I.Y.
Can't remember to change your furnace filter every 3 months? Go to www.3m.com/filtrete, join the Filtrete Clean Air Club and receive free reminders!

Skip it!

WASHABLE OR FIBER-GLASS FURNACE FILTER

THE UGLY

Residents of New York, Oregon, and California face the highest possibility of developing cancer from inhaling toxic chemicals, according to a recent EPA study that reveals air pollution across the nation affecting 2.2 million people.

THE INCONVENIENT TRUTH

Since the 1980s, asthma rates have *doubled* and even quadrupled in some areas of the country! What's more, according to the National Indoor Mold Society, 500,000 people die every year from mold-related deaths.

Sage Advice

Surveys indicate that 41% of homeowners in America neglect to replace their furnace filter every two to three months—and 9% have never changed their filter.

Washable filters can be expensive and high maintenance, and cleaning can cause some particles to end up back in the home.

PORTABLE AIR PURIFIERS

Green it!

LOWE'S IDYLIS™ 200 CADR & 280 CADR AIR PURIFIERS

THE GOOD
Look for an air purifier with carbon and a true HEPA filter like the Lowe's Idylis series. They offer filtration coverage from 155 to 434 square feet. For larger spaces, the IQAir HealthPro Plus provides coverage for 900 square feet or the HM400 by Austin Air filters up to 1,500 square feet and contains a granular carbon/zeolite blend.

- -

THE GREEN
Some portable air purifiers come with energy efficient motors and can definitely save you some green. Great examples are the Lowe's Idylis 200 & 280 CADR units, which are Energy Star certified.

- -

THE CONVENIENT TRUTH
Portable air purifiers are one of the most effective ways to better the indoor air quality of any home or office.

- -

Sage Advice
October 18, 2010 is the date by which the California Air Resources Board requires all portable indoor air cleaning devices sold in California to be certified.

Skip it!
IONIZATION AIR PURIFIER

THE UGLY
Over 22 million Americans suffer from Asthma. What's more, risk studies performed by EPA and its Science Advisory Board (SAB) have consistently ranked indoor air pollution among the top five environmental risks to public health.

THE INCONVENIENT TRUTH
Consumers Union, the publisher of *Consumer Reports*, reported in October 2003 that air ionizers do not perform to high enough standards compared to conventional HEPA air filters.

Healthy Rx
Some ionizing air purifiers emit ozone, the main component of smog! Look for a portable air purifier that has a medical-grade True HEPA filter for certified removal of 99.97% of airborne particles (ex. mold, dust, and pollen) 0.3 microns and larger with carbon. UV-C light to eliminate cold and flu-causing germs or zeolite for the added absorption of chemicals are both great additions.

VACUUMS

Green it!
HOOVER® WIND TUNNEL ANNIVERSARY EDITION U6485-900

THE GOOD

The right vacuum cleaner can be a great way to control indoor allergens. The Hoover® Wind Tunnel U6485-900 proved excellent in cleaning and emissions by third-party testing. Looking for a bagless with a unique feature? The Versatility by Electrolux has a 14-inch telescoping cleaning wand. Both utilize HEPA filtration.

THE GREEN

A HEPA filter is recommended to trap and seal fine particles including dust mites, pollen, ragweed, mold spores, and pet dander. A "true" or "absolute" HEPA will capture particles down to 0.3 microns in size at 99.97% efficiency.

THE CONVENIENT TRUTH

The EPA recommends vacuuming carpet and fabric-covered furniture with vacuums that have high-efficiency filters as a good step to help reduce dust build-up in homes. The good news is that there are now many healthy bagless vacuum cleaner options to choose from compared to years past.

Skip it!

NON-HEPA VACUUM

THE UGLY
According to a Massachusetts special legislative report, 50% of all illnesses in the U.S. are caused by indoor air pollution.

THE INCONVENIENT TRUTH
Allergen particles are carried in the air and settle onto furniture and floor surfaces in your home. Some vacuums just spray these allergens back into the air while vacuuming. This can cause allergic reactions and trigger asthma symptoms in some people.

Healthy Rx
Vacuuming once or twice a week is a great way to improve indoor air quality. However, it is highly recommended for people with allergies to wear a dust mask while doing housework that includes vacuuming and dusting.

INDOOR PAINT

Green it!

BENJAMIN MOORE® NATURA™ PAINT / SHERWIN WILLIAMS® HARMONY®/ AFM SAFE-COAT® ZERO VOC / MYTHIC™ PAINT

THE GOOD
Zero and Low VOC paint help reduce indoor air pollution.

THE GREEN
Some paint manufacturers such as AFM eliminate toxic ingredients such as solvents, heavy metals, chemical residuals, formaldehyde, and other harmful preservatives from their Zero VOC paint.

THE CONVENIENT TRUTH
Low VOC stains and paints have not only become more affordable, but the products themselves are of high quality, durable, and readily available.

Sage Advice
Many people have an allergic reaction to the VOCs that paint emits. The reactions can be anything from mild to life threatening. Mythic Paint is the first high performance paint that guarantees zero VOCs and zero-carcinogens.

Healthy Rx

Unlike upper level ozone, which forms a protective barrier, ground level ozone, commonly called smog, is formed by VOCs and nitrogen oxide (NOx) in the presence of sunlight. At ground level, ozone adversely affects human health and damages vegetation and many common materials.

Skip it!

TRADITIONAL VOC PAINT

THE UGLY

Homes that were painted before 1978 may contain lead paint. Make sure to test for lead prior to stripping or sanding. These actions can release fine lead dust into the air.

THE INCONVENIENT TRUTH

The EPA states that, on average, air pollutants can be 2 to 5 times higher *in* homes than outdoors.

HOME FURNISHINGS

Green it!

FREECYCLE.ORG™

THE GOOD

Join the almost 7 million members worldwide at the Freecycle Network. This non-profit group connects people via its online community, and allows them to give or receive free unwanted stuff in their own towns. The concept of Freecycle spreads over 85 countries, where there are thousands of local groups that represent its millions of members.

THE GREEN

When you Freecycle, you help to reduce waste and save precious resources.

THE CONVENIENT TRUTH

Currently the Freecycle concept keeps over 500 tons of material a day out of landfills.

Sage Advice
Membership is free! Visit freecycle.org.

AND MORE

Sage Advice
The Great Wall of China and the Fresh Kills landfill in New Jersey are the only two manmade structures on Earth that are large enough to be seen from outer space.

Skip it!
MEGA STORE OR MALL

THE UGLY
North America and Western Europe account for 60% of private consumption spending, but only represent a little over one-tenth of the world's population.

THE INCONVENIENT TRUTH
According to World Watch Institute, in 2002, 61% of U.S. credit card users carried a monthly balance, averaging $12,000 at 16% interest. The finance charges on this debt alone are higher that the average per capita income of 35 countries (in purchasing power parity).

LIGHTBULBS
Green it!
LED LIGHT BULB

THE GOOD
LEDs (light emitting diode) use about one-tenth of the energy of an incandescent bulb and about one-half of the CFLs.

THE GREEN
You can cut down on electric bills by using light-emitting diode, LED bulbs instead of the more popular, energy-efficient, compact fluorescent bulbs (CFLs) or incandescents.

THE CONVENIENT TRUTH
Although LEDs are initially more expensive, swapping out incandescent bulbs can save lots of green over their lifetime.

Ron's Green $$ Tip
Artificial lighting accounts for 29% of office energy use. Use the LED calculator at www.led waves.com/led-calc to find your household or office savings. The higher price of the LED bulb translates to a longer lifespan, lasting 60,000 hours compared to incandescents' 1,500 and CFL's 10,000 hours.

Skip it!
CFL & INCANDESCENT LIGHTBULBS

THE UGLY

The new energy-saving light bulbs on the market contain small amounts of mercury. Called "compact fluorescent light bulbs" or CFLs, these bulbs must be disposed of at a facility that accepts toxic waste.

THE INCONVENIENT TRUTH

It is illegal to merely throw CFLs out with your household trash. (some home improvement stores have recycling programs for unbroken CFLs.)

The EPA has some fairly extensive steps, found at www.epa.gov/mercury/spills—for mercury removal after a bulb is broken.

Mother Knows Best!

Steps during a CFL break include: 1) Open a window and leave the room for 15 minutes or more. 2) Shut off the air-conditioning system. 3) Scoop up glass pieces and powder using stiff paper or cardboard and place in a jar with metal lid or a sealed plastic bag. 4) Use sticky tape to pick up any remaining small glass fragments and powder.

CANDLES
Green it!
GREEN NEST
SOY CANDLE

THE GOOD
Green Nest candles use EcoSoya wax, which is 100% vegetable wax, are created with pure soybean oil, and do not contain petroleum, paraffin, pesticides, herbicides, or toxic materials, are *not* subject to animal testing, and are unscented for those with sensitivities.

THE GREEN
The Green Nest candles are bio-degradable, and the ingredients are produced from a renewable, sustainable soy wax that encourages growth without degrading the nutrient-rich soils.

THE CONVENIENT TRUTH
Worried about lead in your candles? Members of the National Candle Association voluntarily agreed not to use lead wicks in 1974, however the CPSC did not place the ban until 2003. Though lead free today, candles brought in from another country or purchased prior to 2003 may be of concern.

Sage Advice
All EcoSoya waxes are manufactured to meet FDA and Kosher standards, contain no GMM (Genetically Modified Material), and are considered GRAS (generally regarded as safe) under the Food, Drug and Cosmetic Act, assuring you will know the FDA has tested and passed the substance for use by people.

Skip it!
PARAFFIN WAX FRAGRANCED CANDLE

THE UGLY

According to the National Candle Association, paraffin (petroleum made from crude oil) is the most commonly used candle wax today. They estimate each year in the U.S., 1 billion pounds of wax is used in the candles sold.

THE INCONVENIENT TRUTH

Federal law requires that candles are labeled with the manufacturer's name, location, and simple usage and safety information, but not for ingredients such as synthetic dyes or fragrances. Look for those labeled 100% essential oils or unscented.

Healthy Rx

Always trim the wick to one-quarter inch before every use to avoid small amounts of soot (ie: unburned carbon particles) from escaping as visible smoke. Candles will soot if the flame is disturbed. Remember to buy candles with cotton wicks and vegetable waxes such as soy or beeswax. Also, verify they have been tested by a third-party accredited laboratory for pesticides, herbicides, and GMMs. Even many soy wax candles still contain pesticides and genetically modified soy.

WATER FILTRATION

Green it!

BRITA® AQUALUX CARAFE / PUR® HORIZONTAL FM9400 FAUCET MOUNT

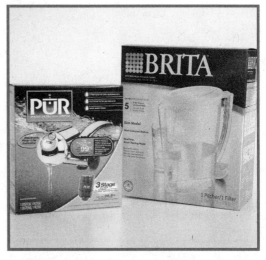

THE GOOD

Most drinking-water filters utilize activated carbon granules that act like a sponge, sucking up that chlorine taste and odor. Brita pitchers can reduce impurities of copper, mercury, cadmium, and zinc in your drinking water.

THE GREEN

Drinking water from a home filter is less expensive than bottled water and helps protect the environment.

THE CONVENIENT TRUTH

One of the most important functions of water in your body is to flush out toxins and salt.

Lisa's D.I.Y.

No filter will give you consistently good performance over the long term unless it receives regular maintenance. As contaminants build up, a filter can not only become less effective, but actually can make your water worse by starting to release harmful bacteria or chemicals back into your filtered water.

Skip it!

POOR CONTAMINANT REMOVAL AND OZONE GENERATING WATER FILTERS

THE UGLY

Many products filter out particles in the water and kill some parasites and bacteria—but they generally fail to remove 21st-century contaminants like pesticides, industrial chemicals, and arsenic. In 2007, third-party testing revealed concerns including clogs, leaks, and high levels of ozone.

THE INCONVENIENT TRUTH

Pregnant women, young children, the elderly, and people with compromised immune systems are particularly vulnerable to some contaminants in tap water.

Healthy Rx

If you're shopping for a water filter, first find out what pollutants might be in your water. While the NSF certification program is not flawless, it does provide assurance that at least some claims made by the manufacturer have been verified. NSF-certified filters have been independently tested to show that they can reduce levels of certain pollutants under specified conditions.

WATER FILTRATION

Green it!

REVERSE OSMOSIS AND DISTILLER

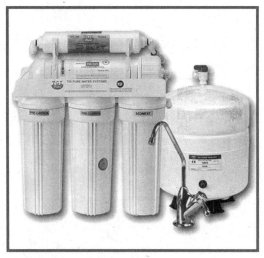

THE GOOD

Using either reverse osmosis or distillation water filtration will reduce fluoride, lead, mercury, and other contaminants in your tap water, which carbon base filters alone do not remove.

THE GREEN

Distillation or reverse osmosis combined with a carbon filter offers the best protection against the widest range of contaminants in your water. The combination of filters help reduce aluminum, arsenic, asbestos, benzene, cholroamine, copper, MTBEs, peticides, THMs, VOCs, and more from your drinking water.

THE CONVENIENT TRUTH

Drinking filtered water will not only prevent ingestion of chlorine, but also its toxic byproducts like trihalomethanes, or THMs. According to research from more than 12 epidemiological studies, these may cause more than 10,000 cases of bladder and rectal cancer each year.

Skip it!

TAP WATER

THE UGLY

Fluoride has been linked to many serious health problems, including bone cancer. The main fluoride chemical added to water (hydofluorosilicic acid) is an industrial by-product from the phosphate fertilizer industry. Unfortunately, every day, over 150 million people drink fluoride from their tap water and they do not even realize it. When ingesting fluoride, almost 93% is absorbed into the bloodstream and whatever is not excreted ends up being deposited into teeth and bones.

- -

THE INCONVENIENT TRUTH

According to the Center of Disease Control, nearly 1 million people get sick from drinking contaminated water each year.

- -

Healthy Rx

Eight glasses of purified water a day will aid your body's ability to properly digest, transport nutrients, remove toxins and waste, lubricate joints, and improve overall immune function.

BATHING
Green it!
SHOWER

THE GOOD
Using "low flow" shower head fixtures restricts the water output to no more than 2.5 gallons per minute (gpm), the federally mandated limit for new fixtures.

THE GREEN
The EPA has launched a water- and energy-saving certification for bathroom fixtures—it's called Water Sense.

THE CONVENIENT TRUTH
Turn off the water when rinsing dishes or brushing teeth and save 2 to 2.5 gallons per minute.

Lisa's D.I.Y.
Install aerators with flow restrictors on kitchen and bathroom faucets and save about 4.7 gallons per day. Wash only full loads of clothing and save 15 to 20 gallons per load.

Skip it!
BATH

THE UGLY

A bath requires 30 to 70 gallons of water compared to low-flow shower-heads that use only 25 gallons of water in ten minutes. Older bathroom fixtures cost more money by wasting water with every use. Every person in America uses around 100 gallons of water a day at home, but almost a third of that could be reduced by installing water-efficient fixtures.

Mother Knows Best!

If you must take a bath, fill the bathtub only halfway while bathing and you'll save 15 to 25 gallons per bath.

THE INCONVENIENT TRUTH

Leaking toilets can trickle away 30 to 50 gallons per day per toilet. Fix leaky faucets and save 15 to 20 gallons per leak per day.

SHOWER FILTRATION

Green it!

**AQUASANA®
SPRITE® / FLOWISE
SHOWERHEADS /
AERATOR / SPEAKMAN®
LOW FLOW SHOWERHEAD**

THE GOOD
Low flow showerheads can help you conserve water while bathing.

THE GREEN
By shortening your showers you can save 2.5 gallons of water per minute.

THE CONVENIENT TRUTH
Sprite Shower filters are easy to install and filter both free and combined chlorines, dirt, sediment, odors, hydrogen sulfide, and iron oxides. Aquasana Shower filters help remove chlorine and synthetic chemicals, THMs, and VOCs. Both balance the pH of your water helping hair and skin.

Ron's Green $$ Tip
Aerators blend water and air to help reduce flow without sacrificing pressure. Costing from $0.50 to $3 apiece, the aerator devices are some of the cheapest green gadgets available. Your utility company may even offer you a rebate or hand them out for free!

Skip it!
STANDARD SHOWERHEADS

THE UGLY
Many municipal water supplies use chorine to disinfect water; unfortunately, chlorine and its byproducts have been linked to serious illness like bladder cancer.

THE INCONVENIENT TRUTH
In just one 10-minute shower you can absorb more chlorine than from drinking water from the same source all day. More water contaminants are released into the air of a home from the shower than from any other source.

Healthy Rx
Many fancy and expensive showerheads in the market don't include filters for chlorine reduction. Use a shower filter like the one shown from Aquasana to help remove potential harmful chlorine and by-products from your bathing water.

NONSTICK COOKWARE

Green it!

CUISINART®
GREEN-WARE™ 12-PIECE
COOKWARE SET

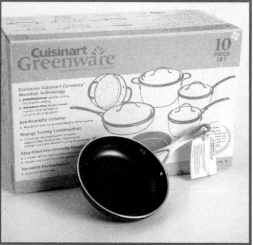

THE GOOD
Cuisinart's Greenware nonstick cookware is made of a PTFE- and PFOA-free nonstick cooking surface, utilizing a hard-anodized pan construction. It provides fast and even heat distribution, with a scratch-resistant nonstick surface that won't peel! For more tips on nonstick cookware, visit: GreenColoredGlasses.net.

THE GREEN
Cuisinart's packaging is made from 100% recycled materials, and printed using 100% biodegradable soy ink. Even the manufacturing gets green kudos for using techniques that reduce harmful carbon emission.

THE CONVENIENT TRUTH
Cuisinart's Greenware is made with 70% recycled steel, and the ceramic-based coating is petroleum free.

Sage Advice
Stuck on nonstick? PFCs—Perflourochemicals (PFOA and PTFE)—are used in the manufacturing of Teflon and in other coated items. They are a likely carcinogen, as they have been shown to cause cancer in animal studies.

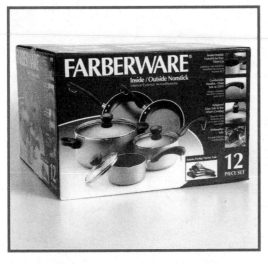

Skip it!

TEFLON 12-PIECE SET

THE UGLY

Teflon and other nonstick pans begin to break down and release toxins into the air at a temperature of only 446° F. According to a Washington, D.C.-based scientific research organization, these pans release a gas that can kill birds and cause flu-like symptoms in humans when they reach normal cooking temperatures.

Sage Advice

PFOA, the chemical used in the manufacturing of non-stick cookware, is actually a breakdown product of PFCs. A highly persistent environmental toxin, it accumulates in the human body over many years, and has been detected in close to 98% of the population tested according to EWG, The Environmental Working Group.

THE INCONVENIENT TRUTH

Teflon is a product name, not a chemical. The chemicals used to make Teflon, PFCs, are present in other non-stick cookware.

MUFFIN PAN
Green it!
LODGE®MUFFIN PAN

THE GOOD
Lodge cast-iron cookware provides unparalleled heating, heat retention, durability, and value against even the most expensive stainless steel cookware.

THE GREEN
Lodge Manufacturing received a Tennessee Governor's Award for Excellence in Hazardous Waste Reduction by switching to an environmentally friendly melting system and recycling their cardboard to reduce new cardboard use by 48.1 tons in 2005.

THE CONVENIENT TRUTH
More than 120 trees have been planted to enhance the beauty and air quality of the Lodge campus. Every 1.4 acres of new tree plantings equals the removal of one motor vehicle from the highway.

Lisa's D.I.Y.

Consumers can help by urging companies to eliminate the use of PFC's and fluorinated alternatives. Tell manufacturers you do not want to be exposed to chemicals that are extremely persistent in the environment, bioaccumulative, and linked to adverse health effects. Demand healthier options that are proven safe.

Skip it!

TEFLON®
MUFFIN PAN

THE UGLY
In a 2007 John Hopkins' Bloomberg School of Public Health study PFOA was detected in 100% of the newborns examined.

THE INCONVENIENT TRUTH
A study from UCLA has linked Teflon cookware, more specifically the PFCs in Teflon, to female infertility.

Sage Advice

Lodge Manufacturing, in coordination with the government of Marion County, Tennessee, made three storm-water settling ponds to support plant and animal life. The county saved $191,311.75 by using 9,225 cubic yards of foundry sand for the required 12-inch protective.

Combined efforts created a policy for non-hazardous foundry sand adopted in April 1996. Together, a great example of industry and government working together for good of the environment has been achieved through Lodge's efforts.

GRILL PAN
Green it!

LE CREUSET®
GRILL PAN

THE GOOD
Le Creuset enameled cast-iron cookware styles are cast in their own sand molds, which are broken after casting and reused again, creating uniqueness for each item.

THE GREEN
Energy efficient cookware? It's true! Once hot, Le Creuset's cookware requires only a low to medium heat setting to maintain a good cooking performance and allows the food to continue cooking even when removed from the heat source.

THE CONVENIENT TRUTH
Since Roman times, cast iron has represented the preferred material for cooking pots, and it is still forged and crafted by hand today, maintaining evenly proportioned heat.

Sage Advice
The vitreous enamel cooking surface of Le Creuset's cookware is hygienic and impervious to flavors and odors, and distributes heat more evenly, preventing hot spots. Easily being cleaned by hand or dishwasher, the cookware is also suitable for marinating or for storing raw or cooked foods in the refrigerator or freezer.

Skip it!
TEFLON GRILL PAN

THE UGLY
Health and environmental concerns have been raised regarding PFCs (Per-fluorinated compounds) from many scientists due to their persistent, bioaccumulative, and toxic nature.

THE INCONVENIENT TRUTH
Studies by the CDC, and others, have found PFCs in humans throughout the U.S. and the world that are known to have crossed the placenta, directly exposing the developing fetus.

Healthy Rx
The EPA's Science Advisory Board considers PFOA (a class of PFs) a likely carcinogen. While eight of the companies currently using PFOA have voluntarily agreed to reduce PFOA releases by 2010, they are not required to eliminate them until 2015.

LOAF PAN

Green it!

WILLIAMS SONOMA®
EMILE HENRY
ARTISAN LOAF PAN

THE GOOD
Err on the side of caution and stick with glass, earthenware, or cast iron for baking.

THE GREEN
Since 1850, Emile Henry's ceramic bake ware has been made from high-fired Burgundy clay having no lead or cadmium. All of the glazes meet California Prop 65 and are 100% food safe.

THE CONVENIENT TRUTH
The earthenware pan offers superb heat conduction and retention and is very strong. The pan bakes evenly and stays hot at the table, while being safe for oven or broiler use. It even goes directly from freezer to oven.

Sage Advice
In 2004, aluminum cookware accounted for nearly $500 million in sales, according to the Cookware Manufacturers Association. Avoid direct food contact with aluminum—especially with acidic foods as the aluminum salts from cookware can leach from the pot into the food being cooked. Look for anodized aluminum instead.

Skip It!
NONSTICK
LOAF PAN

THE UGLY
PFCs are manmade compounds, based on the element fluorine. And it isn't just found in cookware. They are widely used to create water- and stain-resistant treatments for household furnishing such as fabric, furniture, and carpet. (Do the names Teflon and Stainmaster ring a bell?)

THE INCONVENIENT TRUTH
Stick with "unstick." Buyers beware of newer, replacement chemicals for non-stick. According to a report in 2008, the manufacturers' own tests showed that many of the alternative PFC chemicals lead "to a conclusion of substantial risk to human health or to the environment."

Sage Advice
PFC's have been found in some Chicago Metallic Silverstone loaf pans as revealed in tests by the EWG. PFCs are linked with developmental toxicity, cancer, thyroid, liver and immune system functions, cholesterol increases, and low birth measurements in newborn humans as evidenced in scientific studies.

FOOD STORAGE

Green It!

PRESERVE® PLASTIC STORAGE CONTAINERS / CORNINGWARE / PYREX®

THE GOOD
When purchasing containers for food or beverages, look for the resin identification code (usually on the bottom) on the packaging. Numbers 2, 4, and 5 are your allies. Enemies are numbers 3, 6, and 7. Number 1 is fine for single use and widely accepted by municipal recyclers.

THE GREEN
Choose safer plastics, glass, or ceramic for food storage—especially with hot food items.

THE CONVENIENT TRUTH
The dawn of the plastic era was in the 1950s. This was when plastic for consumer goods started to be used on a mass scale.

Sage Advice
It is estimated each plastic item could last in the environment anywhere between 400 to 1,000 years. Plastic also becomes brittle when recycled, unlike glass which can be recycled 25 to 30 times.

THE INCONVENIENT TRUTH

Plastics do not naturally biodegrade. Instead, plastics require the sun's ultraviolet rays to break down into smaller and smaller toxic bits, which in turn contaminate soil, waterways, and oceans. Many of the animals drinking from these waterways and living in these oceans are caught and eaten by us, therefore passing on the toxins.

Skip It!

PLASTIC CONTAINERS: #3 PVC, V, VINYL; #6 PS; OR #7 POLYCARBONATE

THE UGLY

Presently, the world produces 200 million tons of plastic a year and 96% of that is not recycled. It gets uglier: 8% of the entire world's oil production is used in manufacturing plastic.

Double trouble: the world's plastic manufacturing doubles in quantity every 20 years. This is equal to a rate of 3.5% every year! Plastic production creates 100 times more toxic emissions than glass and can potentially contaminate the product it holds.

MOVING BOXES

Green It!

USED CARDBOARD BOXES

THE GOOD

The average U.S. citizen creates 4.39 pounds of trash *per day*. Companies like Earth Friendly Moving in California are putting some of that trash to use. They offer a comprehensive, zero-waste pack and move solution. One of their moving boxes, called the "Recopack" is made from 100% hard to recycle plastic trash mined from local landfills.

THE GREEN

Are some recycled moving boxes prematurely terminated? Not at UsedCardboardBoxes.com! They rescue quality used boxes from large companies that might otherwise have just been thrown away. If the rescued boxes meet their strict requirements for quality, shape, and strength, they are pre-packed and offered in low-cost, earth-friendly stacks to their customers.

THE CONVENIENT TRUTH

Nine cubic yards of landfill space and 46 gallons of oil are saved by every one ton of cardboard that is recycled.

Sage Advice

Cardboard is used to ship 90% of all products in the U.S. according to Earth911.org.

Skip It!
NEW BOXES

THE UGLY
Packaging makes up one-third of the waste generated the United States.

THE INCONVENIENT TRUTH
Every day, the U.S. throws away enough trash to fill 63,000 garbage trucks.

Mother Knows Best!
There is no reason to buy new moving boxes when you have many other options. For example, at the U-Haul Box Exchange message board you can actually trade, sell, or buy reusable boxes and other moving supplies with other U-Haul customers.

PAPER TOWELS

Green It!

MARCAL® / SEVENTH GENERATION® / EARTH FRIENDLY®

THE GOOD
Marcal has led the way in the recycling industry, having produced recycled paper products for over 50 years.

THE GREEN
According to Greenpeace, "Recycled tissue products help protect ancient forests, clean water, and wildlife habitat. It's easier on the Earth to make tissues from paper instead of trees."

THE CONVENIENT TRUTH
Earth Friendly and Marcal Small Steps paper products are all produced with 100% recycled paper.

Sage Advice
Seventh Generation, Earth Friendly, and Marcal bathroom toilet sheets and paper towels are made from paper that is whitened without chlorine. They are also hypo-allergenic, contain no added dyes and fragrances and are unscented.

Skip It!
VIRGIN WOOD PAPER TOWELS

THE UGLY
Most paper towels are made from virgin wood pulp that has been bleached and dyed.

- -

THE INCONVENIENT TRUTH
Over 3,000 inconvenient tons of paper towels are sent to the landfill *each day.*

- -

Mother Knows Best!
When purchasing paper towels, don't settle for anything less than 100% recycled content. Many popular regular brands don't even offer recycled content in the product and if they do it is much less than 100%. You should also avoid regular brands that use chlorine to whiten their products.

You can also offset some of your paper towel use with reusable cloth napkins and microfiber cloths when possible.

TOILET TISSUE

Green It!

GREEN FOREST® / SEVENTH GENERATION®

THE GOOD

No greenwashing here. Green Forest's tissue is made from 100% recycled paper, with a minimum 90% post consumer content and is chlorine free! Always avoid tissue containing bleach and fragrances!

- -

THE GREEN

Green Forest, Seventh Generation, Earth Friendly, Nature Value, and Marcal products don't destroy trees! They've reduced landfill accumulation by making their paper products from recycled paper.

- -

THE CONVENIENT TRUTH

Seventh Generation's toilet tissue has new and improved softness and is safe for low-flow toilets.

- -

Sage Advice

Avoid bleached products. Charmin and Scott brands use chlorine compounds in the bleaching process, which, as Greenpeace points out, emits carcinogens. Look for Scott Naturals new line as a better option.

Skip It!
VIRGIN WOOD TOILET TISSUE

THE UGLY
In the paper making process, wood is ground, pressed, dried, and chlorine bleached. Over 1,000 different *organochlorines*, including the carcinogen dioxin and mercury are present. Dioxin is one of the nastiest substances in existence formed as a by-product of the manufacture of organic chemicals and plastics that contain chlorine.

THE INCONVENIENT TRUTH
In 2005, nearly 35% of the U.S. generated 246 million tons of municipal solid waste was paper. Nearly half of the trees cut in North America are used to make paper.

Mother Knows Best!
The nonprofit, Natural Resources Defense Council, avows forests at home and abroad are being destroyed to make toilet paper, facial tissues, paper towels and other disposable paper products. The destruction of our continent's most vibrant forests by major paper producers such as Scott, Cottonelle, Kleenex, Viva, Charmin, Bounty, and Quilted Northern continues today.

FOOD WRAP

Green It!

REYNOLDS WRAP®
100% RECYCLED
ALUMINUM FOIL

THE GOOD

Recycling aluminum can save 80% of the energy required to generate aluminum from raw material and it produces fewer emissions like greenhouse gases, while reducing waste sent to a landfill.

THE GREEN

Reynolds Wrap foil utilizes 100% recycled aluminum and 100% recycled paperboard packaging, including water-based inks and food-safe foil made from a mix of pre and post-consumer aluminum. It can also be recycled.

THE CONVENIENT TRUTH

Also check out If You Care aluminum foil. It is made from 100% recycled aluminum and can be recycled again.

If you're a baker, they offer unbleached paper baking cups. Because they are unbleached, there is no chlorine used in the production.

Lisa's D.I.Y.

At Reynoldsrecycled.com, they offer many clever uses when cooking. For one, try crumpled pieces of Reynolds Wrap aluminum foil as a scouring pad to clean barbecue grill grates. It makes it a breeze to keep your grill clean between uses.

Skip It!
PLASTIC WRAP

THE UGLY
Glad Cling Wrap, like Saran Premium Wrap, does not contain polyvinylidene chloride (PVdC). However, both still utilize petroleum in their production. What's more, plastic wrap doesn't withstand heat and cold as well as aluminum foil.

THE INCONVENIENT TRUTH
In just one year, Americans make enough plastic film to shrink-wrap the entire state of Texas.

Healthy Rx
Recycled aluminum foil is as clean and safe to use with food as foil made from new aluminum, also referred to as virgin aluminum. Recycled aluminum requires heating the metal to more than 1,200°F, burning off any debris and turning it into a molten liquid, which is then sent through a filtration process, poured and rolled into thin sheets.

BLEACH

Green It!

SEVENTH GENERATION® CHLORINE-FREE BLEACH

THE GOOD

Other healthy bleach options include: Ecover Non Chlorine Bleach or 20 Mule Team Borax. You'll want to keep Borax around—it is also great on surfaces and as a deodorizer.

- -

THE GREEN

Seventh Generation's Chlorine Free Bleach is free of chlorine, dyes, and fragrances and utilizes natural oxygen bleach (hydrogen peroxide) and deionized H_2O. Great for the planet because it degrades into oxygen and water.

- -

THE CONVENIENT TRUTH

Avoid bleach in your laundry, since chlorine is listed as a hazardous air pollutant in the 1990 Clean Air Act.

- -

Lisa's D.I.Y.

Make your laundry brighter and whiter by adding these ingredients to your washing load: ¼ cup of borax or ½ cup of washing soda. Or add ¼ cup lemon juice in the rinse cycle for a bleach alternative. For an easy nontoxic fabric softener, add ¼ cup of white vinegar to the rinse cycle. Hanging your clothes out to dry is the best way to get a fresh smell and whiter whites.

Skip It!
BLEACH

THE UGLY
Chlorine—otherwise known as sodium hypochlorite, hypochlorite, hydrogen chloride, or hydrochloric acid—is a respiratory irritant, which can aggravate asthma, emphysema, or chronic bronchitis, and can be fatal when inhaled.

THE INCONVENIENT TRUTH
Say goodbye to chlorine bleach. Why? Contact can cause severe damage to eyes, skin, mouth, and throat; can cause liver and kidney damage; and causes more poisoning exposures than any household chemical!

Sage Advice
Chlorine and ammonia (found in many window, floor and jewelry cleaning products), when combined, form a deadly, lung damaging gas—chloramine gas. Exposure to this causes irritation to the eyes, nose, throat, and airways. Symptoms include teary eyes, runny nose, sore throat, coughing, and chest congestion.

ALL-PURPOSE CLEANER

Green It!

GREEN NEST® / SEVENTH GENERATION® FREE AND CLEAR® / MRS. MEYERS® / ECO-ME® HOME KIT

THE GOOD

Looking for cleaners truly free of fragrances, dyes, and masking agents? Try The Green Nest All Purpose Cleaner at only $1.13/quart. Environmentally safer and nontoxic, it's also approved by the South Coast Air Quality Management District.

Desire a sweeter smell? Mrs. Myers, Eco-Me, and Method products have great smells. All of these are biodegradable and use plant surfactants rather than harsh chemicals!

THE GREEN

Support companies making healthier products and don't rely on just the ingredient labels or clever marketing. The U.S. Federal Code of Regulations exempts manufacturers from full labeling of products if used for personal, family, or household use.

THE CONVENIENT TRUTH

A little upfront investment can save you later. According to government statistics, in 2005, people in America spent $11 billion on doctors' bills, prescription medicines, and other allergy remedies.

Skip It!

NONBIODEGRADABLE CLEANERS

THE UGLY

The National Research Council estimates that fewer than 30% of the roughly 17,000 petrochemicals available for home use are tested for their effects on human and environmental health.

THE INCONVENIENT TRUTH

According to the CDC, asthma rates have doubled over the last 20 years. Indoor air pollutants can trigger asthma attacks.

The Consumer Product Safety Commission connects 150 chemicals commonly found in our homes to allergies, birth defects, cancer and psychological disorders.

Sage Advice

Exposure to high levels of toxic air pollutants can cause many adverse health effects. Some of these health problems include damage to the immune system, neurological, developmental, and respiratory issues, and even cancer.

Indoor air quality in homes is not regulated by the United States government. The Consumer Product Safety Commission connects 150 chemicals commonly found in our homes to allergies, birth defects, cancer and psychological disorders.

DISHWASHING DETERGENT
Green It!

BIOKLEEN® WITH NATURAL OXYGEN BLEACH / ECOVER® TABLETS

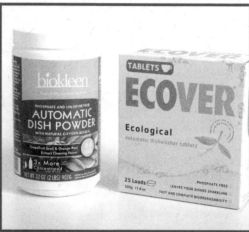

THE GOOD
Look for phosphate-free detergents with enzymes and avoid products that contain dyes and perfumes.

THE GREEN
Ecover tablets utilize plant-based ingredients and offer quick and complete biodegradability. Biokleen is fragrance free, and is clear of dyes and brighteners.

THE CONVENIENT TRUTH
Avoid chlorine-based cleaning agents. Chlorine fumes from steam can leach from your dishwasher. It can cause eye and skin irritation as well as difficulty breathing.

Sage Advice
Approximately 80,000 industrial chemicals are registered for use in the U.S. in all of the products we eat, touch, wear, and use to furnish our homes, but that fewer than 20% have been tested for their impact on human health and the environment!

Skip It!

NONBIODEGRADABLE DETERGENT WITH PHOS-PHATES

THE UGLY

Most household cleaning products contain poisonous chemicals and harsh corrosives that can be flammable. Improper disposal can not only harm you, but precious wildlife too, as these chemicals can contaminate both soil and water.

Mother Knows Best!

Avoid half full: run the dishwasher only when full and save 2 to 4.5 gallons per load.

THE INCONVENIENT TRUTH

Avoid products containing ammonia, formaldehyde, or phosphates. Phosphates are used in dishwashing detergents. They are water-softening mineral additives. When they leach into waterways, they encourage algae growth. This, in turn, suffocates aquatic life. They can also cause severe skin irritation and if ingested, can cause nausea, vomiting and diarrhea.

LAUNDRY DETERGENT

Green It!

TRADER JOE'S® LAUNDRY DETERGENT / ECOS® FREE AND CLEAR

THE GOOD
The U.S. / Canadian Commission has put up a call to ban bleach in North America.

THE GREEN
Trader Joe's detergent is free of phosphates, contains zero chlorine bleach, uses a cellulose optical brightener, and is 100% biodegradable. Lavender oil is added for scent.

THE CONVENIENT TRUTH
Ecos concentrated detergent is made with plant based surfactants. It has a built-in soy based fabric softener and cellulose based, versus as synthetic or petroleum optical brightener. It's nontoxic, biodegradable, and safe for the environment!

Sage Advice

Although phosphates have been phased out of laundry detergents, other laundry chemicals are a cause for concern, especially nonylphenol ethoxylates (NPEs). NPEs are surfactants which help other ingredients penetrate dirt and grime, but unfortunately belong to a group of hormone-disrupting compounds called alkylphenol ethoxylates (APEs).

Sage Advice

Avoid NPEs in laundry detergents. Nonylphenol ethoxylates are recognized by the Environmental Protection Agency as toxic to aquatic plants and animals.

Skip It!

NONBIODEGRADABLE LAUNDRY DETERGENT

THE UGLY

Over 12 million school days are lost each year due to asthma attacks, according to the American Lung Association.

THE INCONVENIENT TRUTH

Connections are being made between bleach and the increasing occurrences of breast cancer in women, learning and behavioral troubles in children, and reproductive issues in men.

BBQ GRILL CLEANER

Green It!

SIMPLE GREEN®
BBQ GRILL CLEANER

THE GOOD

You are what you eat. When cleaning your barbeque or grill of food particles and baked on grease, be cognizant of what you are using to clean it. There are great nontoxic cleaning degreasers on the market today. Don't use harsh, toxic grill cleaners that may come in contact with future meals you are making.

THE GREEN

Simple Green Heavy Duty BBQ and Grill Cleaner is a great example of an environmentally responsible choice you can make when purchasing a degreaser for your grill. It contains biodegradable cleaning power and even comes in a can that is 100% recyclable.

THE CONVENIENT TRUTH

Propane burns cleaner than other natural fuel sources like wood and charcoal. When you use propane, your barbeque will produce less smoke and the fire is easier to maintain.

Sage Advice

You can even clean your grill's range hoods, vents, filters, and cooking utensils with Simple Green BBQ cleaner.

Skip It!

NONBIODEGRADABLE BBQ CLEANER

THE UGLY
Regardless of what barbeque cleaner you use, when cooking on a charcoal grill, the smoke from the grill will emit toxic VOCs (Volatile Organic Compounds).

THE INCONVENIENT TRUTH
Charcoal grills produce twice as much CO_2 as a gas barbeque grill.

Sage Advice
Some grill cleaners contain harsh chemicals that could not only endanger your health over time, but also damage the environment.

DIAPERS

Green It!

HUGGIES® PURE AND NATURAL / G DIAPERS® STARTER KIT

THE GOOD

Earth friendly gDiapers are comprised of almost all natural materials and the inserts, which are made mostly of fluffed wood pulp, can be flushed straight down the toilet. Get started with a kit containing washable cloth pants and snap-in liners.

THE GREEN

Switch to cloth diapers and help save our landfills. As an added bonus, cloth diapers are not full of elemental chlorine or plastics. The gDiapers need far less washing than regular cloth diapers.

THE CONVENIENT TRUTH

No more fighting over whose turn it is to deal with the dirty diaper! Most diaper services pick up once a week and will exchange your dirties with a fresh clean set of diapers. Check with the National Association of Diaper Services (diapernet.org) to find one in your area.

Lisa's D.I.Y.

Still want to contribute to the 18 billion disposable diapers that are thrown away each year? At least opt for a safe brand for your baby like Huggies Pure and Natural, which are made with organic cotton and aloe vera, and are fragrance free and hypoallergenic. Or try Nature Boy and Girl, a biodegradable version.

Skip It!
DISPOSABLE PLASTIC DIAPERS

THE UGLY
Not only do diapers fill up our landfills, they can take up to 500 years to decompose.

THE INCONVENIENT TRUTH
With just a temporary inconvenience, be diaper free. Known as "elimination communication," a method of natural infant hygiene and infant potty training, your baby can be trained in as little as a year and a half.

Sage Advice
You'll have spent $2,000 after your child uses the typical 8,000 to 10,000 disposable diapers before being potty trained. In the United States alone, we pay an average of $350 million annually to deal with diaper disposal.

BABY DIAPER CREAM

Green It!

EARTH MAMA-ANGEL® BABY / CAROL'S DAUGHTER® / TERRESSENTIALS®

THE GOOD
Earth Mama-Angel Baby bottom balm is better for baby. It's allergy tested, non-irritating, vegan, and made with organic olive oil infused with antibacterial and antifungal organic herbs, shea butter, and pure essential oils.

THE GREEN
Children are more affected by toxins than adults, as they breathe more air pound for pound. Almost 60% of what you rub onto a baby's skin is absorbed and can be detected in the blood within minutes.

THE CONVENIENT TRUTH
Also look for Carol's Daughter Body Jelly with 0% petroleum. Or, try Terressentials Terrefic Tush Diaper Cream

with 100% certified organic ingredients or Earth Tribe Kids Baby Balm.

Lisa's D.I.Y.
With just a spray bottle of water and a few dozen washcloths, you can make your own supply of diaper wipes and avoid the alcohol and fragrances in disposable baby wipes that can irritate sensitive baby skin. Keep damp washcloths in a zip lock bag for on-the-go ease.

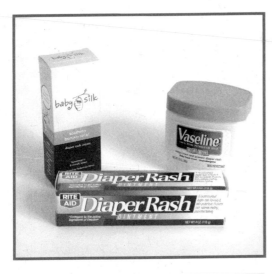

Healthy Rx

Fabric softeners and anti-static products can leave irritating residues behind on baby's soft skin. Use safe solutions like Terraessentials; they are 100% organic, utilizing an ayurvedic "skin healer" of organic centella asiatica infused in organic oils and butters. Avoid petroleum jelly.

Skip It!

CHEMICAL- OR PETROLEUM-BASED DIAPER CREAM

THE UGLY

Residues of strong detergents can cause a rash. Use fragrance- and dye-free detergents for washing and soothing.

THE INCONVENIENT TRUTH

Avoid culprits hiding in your diaper cream such as: BHA (a possible carcinogen), Boric Acid, Sodium borate, Fragrances, Ceteareth 5 and 20, PEG 8, Petrolatum, Propylene Glycol, Parabens, and Mineral Oil.

BABY POWDER

Green It!

JASCO® ORGANICS VELVET NATURAL BABY POWDER / BABY ORGANIC® COCONUT BABY POWDER

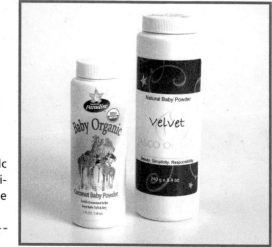

THE GOOD
Jasco's powder does not contain talc or fragrance. It's vegan, with no animal testing and over 95% of the ingredients are organic.

- -

THE GREEN
Make your own powder with cornstarch and essential oils and prevent talc from being mined since talc miners have increased risk of lung cancer.

- -

THE CONVENIENT TRUTH
Baby Organics powder contains only organic coconut powder & and organic arrowroot powder. It is USDA organic, vegan and soy free.

- -

Mother Knows Best!
Moms across America knew prior to the early 1970s the convenience of cloth—it's easier to verify if your baby is wet with cloth diapers, since disposables actually absorb moisture into the diaper. Unfortunately, the bacteria contributing to diaper rash are still in contact with baby's skin.

Healthy Rx

Shop for powders that do not contain the following suspect ingredients or preservatives:

- **DMDM Hydantoin:** Allergen and irritant that can form cancer-causing contaminants.
- **Sodium Borate:** The cosmetic industry's own safety advisory panel says is unsafe for infants and cautions against its use.
- **Fragrance:** Allergens that may contain neurotoxic or hormone-disrupting chemicals.

Skip It!

NONORGANIC BABY POWDER

THE UGLY

Avoid use of talcum powder. Long-term use of talc has been linked to ovarian cancer in women, and tiny airborne particles from baby powder can damage the developing lungs of an infant.

THE INCONVENIENT TRUTH

More than 49 million diapers per day are being used in America. This equates to 570 diapers per second—that's a lot of baby powder!

LUNCH BOXES

Green It!

CLOTH REUSABLE LUNCH BOXES / LUNCH BAGS

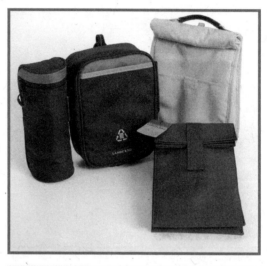

THE GOOD
Use cloth bags. Hero Bags are organic cotton lunch bags that are conveniently machine washable.

THE GREEN
Made from recycled juice boxes, Basura Bags are made by a women's cooperative in the Philippines. They are also 100% lead free.

THE CONVENIENT TRUTH
Also machine washable, try Lunchsense that are BPA-, lead-, and PVC-free lunch boxes or To-Go Ware stainless steel lunch containers and carriers at www.to-goware.com.

Ron's Green $$ Tip
Save money and eat healthy by bringing your own lunch. Around 44 million working Americans are buying their lunch or going out to eat each day. Healthy Child Healthy World offers a free colorful download: The Healthy School Lunch Pocket Guide. Parents can slip it in their kid's backpack as a quick reminder for healthier eating options: http://healthychild.org/uploads/File/PocketGuide_Lunches.pdf

Skip It!
VINYL / PVC LUNCH BOXES

THE UGLY

Lead for lunch? A 2006 study reported large amounts of lead showing up in the vinyl lunchboxes that they tested. The highest levels were discovered in the lining of the lunchboxes themselves, which is the worst of all places, since that comes into direct contact with the food.

THE INCONVENIENT TRUTH

Unfortunately, DEHP is a common regular chemical addition to the vinyl used in lunchboxes. DEHP is a phthalate, alleged carcinogen, and reproductive toxicant.

Healthy Rx

One popular lunch box tested for 90 times the allowable limit for lead in paint in children's products. Make sure you are consumer aware. The good news is that there is a great option out there, called LunchBots. It is made from the highest quality 18/8 stainless steel that does not leach chemicals, as many plastic containers do.

HARD TOYS

Green It!

HABA® WOODEN FIRST BLOCKS

THE GOOD
In 2009, the CPS Modernization Act went into effect, restricting the amount of lead, arsenic, cadmium, and mercury in children's products.

THE GREEN
The HABA wooden first blocks don't harm baby or the environment because they're made of maple wood, and coated in natural, water-based, nontoxic paints.

THE CONVENIENT TRUTH
Of 1,500 popular toys tested by HealthyToys.org, 1 in 3 was found to contain significant levels of toxic chemicals such as lead and arsenic. Test at home using safe lead check swabs from www.leadcheck.com.

Lisa's D.I.Y.
In 2007, there were over 12 million toy recalls. Mattel and Fisher recalled nearly 2 million popular toys including Big Bird, Elmo, Dora, Barbie doll accessories, "Sarge" toy cars and more due to excessive levels of lead found in the toys. In 2009, the Daiso Company recalled 130 toys due to excessive lead and phthalates. Visit www. usrecall-news.com or www.cpsc.gov for a current list of lead recalled toys.

Skip It!

IMPORTED TOXIC TOYS

THE UGLY

In third-party, independent studies, Little Tikes bath letters and numbers showed the product contains mercury, a heavy metal that can damage the brain, kidneys, and developing fetus and chromium, which may be linked to cancer and reproductive hazards.

THE INCONVENIENT TRUTH

The current federal Toxic Substances Control Act (TSCA) is considered *one of the weakest environmental laws* in existence today. It allows chemicals into the market with little to no testing and severely limits the EPA's powers to protect public health in this area.

Mother Knows Best!

Avoid products that could contain lead. Poisoning in children can cause neurological damage, reduced IQ, slowed body growth, hearing problems, behavior or attention problems and kidney damage.

SOFT TOYS

Green It!

ORGANIC PLUSH TOYS FROM MIYIM SIMPLY ORGANIC®

THE GOOD
The Kid-Safe Chemicals Act (KSCA) would update and strengthen the Toxic Substances Control Act (TSCA) by requiring that all chemicals be proven safe for children before they can be sold. Go to: ewg.org/kid-safe-chemicals-act-blog/kid-safe-chemicals-act.

THE GREEN
Great news for the state of California: In July 2009, the state Senate passed the Toxics-Free Babies and Toddlers Act.

THE CONVENIENT TRUTH
Effective February 10, 2009, the federal government restricted three types of phthalates permanently, and

placed temporary restrictions on three others.

Sage Advice
The law permanently bans the sale of toys intended for children 12 or younger or child-care articles for children 3 and under that contain more than 0.1% of three phthalates: di(2-ethylhexyl) phthalate (DEHP), dibutyl phthalate (DBP), and butyl benzyl phthalate (BBP).

Skip It!
NONORGANIC PLUSH TOY

THE UGLY
According to a study by the Environmental Working Group, on average babies in the U.S. are born with over 300 industrial chemicals in their bodies. Many of these chemicals are suspected of contributing to health problems. Many are known carcinogens and chemicals that impair brain development.

THE INCONVENIENT TRUTH
Phthlates are a group of chemicals that are used to soften plastic. They can be found everywhere in your home, including teethers, pacifiers, and rattles.

Sage Advice
Hidden chemicals can be found in toys including lead, mercury, cadmium, arsenic, bromine, and phthalates. Studies link phthalate exposure to hormonal changes, birth defects, DNA damage, reduced lung function, and premature puberty. Children typically have greater exposure to phthalates than adults. Other studies link phthalates to reduced sperm quality.

BABY FOOD

Green It!

HAPPY BABY® / GERBER® ORGANICS / PLUM® ORGANICS FROZEN

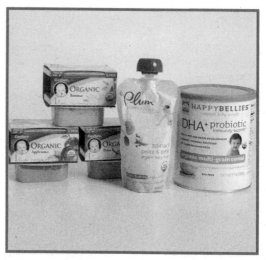

THE GOOD

Plum Organics and Happy Baby have BPA-free packaging. Happy Baby offers Happy Bellies, the *only* organic immunity boosting probiotic dry cereals available with DHA.

THE GREEN

Happy Baby frozen foods are all organic and consist of 100% natural ingredients. They contain zero nuts, soy, dairy, sugar, wheat, pesticides, chemical fertilizers, or GMO—genetically modified organism.

THE CONVENIENT TRUTH

Buying HAPPYBABY food spreads the happiness to feed malnourished children in Malawi through their partner Project Peanut Butter.

Lisa's D.I.Y.

Plum Baby Food is USDA Organic and available for babies, tots, and kids. It contains no high fructose corn syrup, no trans fats, and no artificial ingredients. Or, serve up quality food and save some money by making your own while sneaking healthy foods in your kids meals. Refer to the book *The Sneaky Chef* for great recipes!

Mother Knows Best!

Studies confirm that breast feeding is the best for baby. Although most baby bottle manufacturers agreed to stop using BPA in 2009, it can still be found in other products including canned food linings. The FDA has not banned BPA from baby products on a nationwide level. However FDA considers the safety of BPA to be uncertain.

Skip It!
NONORGANIC BABY FOOD

THE UGLY

Melamine and BPA in your babies' formula more than you bargained for? Bisphenol A (BPA) is a plastic chemical used to make epoxy linings of metal food cans, like those for canned infant formula, which has been linked to hormone disruption.

THE INCONVENIENT TRUTH

Some baby foods tested in The Children's Food Campaign (U.K.) contain as much sugar and saturated fats as chocolate cookies. The Heinz Toddler's Own Mini Cheese Biscuits had more saturated fat per 100g than a McDonald's Quarter Pounder with cheese. Others revealed 29% sugar and trans fats—which are linked to heart disease.

KIDS' PAJAMAS

Green It!

ORGANIC PAJAMAS

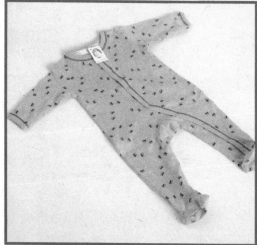

THE GOOD
Sleepwear that fits snugly does not trap the air needed for fabric to burn and reduces the chances of contact with a flame.

THE GREEN
Choose 100% certified organic, snug fitting pajamas that offer fire safety as well as safety for your child, ensuring no added chemicals are present.

THE CONVENIENT TRUTH
There are federal safety guidelines for pajamas made for children in the 9 to 14 months set by the Consumer Product Safety Commission.

Sage Advice
According to the CPSC, sleepwear, including loungewear for children ages 9 to 14 months, must be tight-fitting or made of flame-resistant material to reduce the risk of burns.

Skip It!

SYNTHETIC FABRIC PAJAMAS

THE UGLY

Polyester is derived from crude oil and utilizes more energy than cotton production. It also doesn't breathe, absorb, or release moisture like cotton or wool.

THE INCONVENIENT TRUTH

Although most synthetic fabrics are inherently flame retardant and meet this requirement, the chemicals in the construction of the fabric include halogenated hydrocarbons (chlorine and bromine), inorganic flame retardants (antimony oxides), and phosphate based compounds.

Sage Advice

The CPSC requirements do not apply for infant (0-9 months) sleepwear, since infants are less mobile, and most burn injuries result from children playing with fire.

MOISTURE PAD

Green It!

ORGANIC WOOL MOISTURE PAD

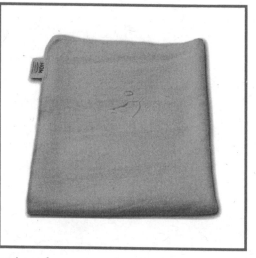

THE GOOD
Wool is naturally flame-retardant, naturally repellent to dust mites, resilient in form and shape, cool in the summer and warm in winter, and absorbent. Wool can absorb 30% moisture and remain dry (not to be confused with waterproof however).

THE GREEN
Happy sheep means happy sleep! Organic farming methods for cotton and wool production guarantee that the crops are free from contaminants such as pesticides, herbicides, and synthetic fertilizers while also protecting the air, water, and wildlife from these chemicals.

THE CONVENIENT TRUTH
Make sure to test for wool allergies and opt for an organic cotton mattress pad if sensitivities to wool are present.

Sage Advice
Green Nest's 100% Pure Wool Moisture Pad is free of chemicals, dyes, and oils, and contains no residues from the processing. It is constructed using only vegetable-based agents for washing, lubrication and static control. It is machine washable and available in two sizes—crib and puddle.

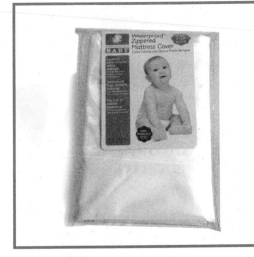

Skip It!

PLASTIC MOISTURE PROTECTOR

THE UGLY

What's your baby breathing in? Synthetic fabrics like polyester and PVC are made from petrochemicals. Covers with water, stain, wrinkle resistant, and flame-retardant chemicals can off-gas VOCs like formaldehyde.

THE INCONVENIENT TRUTH

Plastic mattress covers are designed with the mattress in mind, not your baby. Pure Wool (100%) is recommended because it provides excellent protection for your baby's mattress. Wool is naturally water resistant and dries quickly, so it is good for protecting against accidents.

Mother Knows Best!

An organic mattress protector will consist of undyed or naturally dyed fibers instead of petroleum-based dyes and no pesticides, petroleum-based plastics, or dangerous chemicals. However, there are mattresses made with organic cotton and waterproof material such as food-grade polyethylene.

PET BED

Green It!
GREEN NEST
ORGANIC PET BED

THE GOOD
Organic pet beds contain organic cotton, natural rubber, and wool to keep moisture at bay and prevent mildew.

THE GREEN
Pamper your pooch! Just as you shop for an organic cotton or natural rubber pillow for yourself, look for these same qualities in a pet bed. The Green Nest Organic Pet Bed uses natural rubber for the core support, giving it outstanding heat and moisture regulation, and of course the added benefit of a natural dust-mite repellant from the Hevea milk in the rubber.

THE CONVENIENT TRUTH
Shredded natural rubber or wool bedding conform to your pet's shape and reduces their pain pressure points.

Sage Advice
Some organic pet beds are filled with natural lavender-scented buckwheat hulls or stuffing made of recycled plastic bottles.

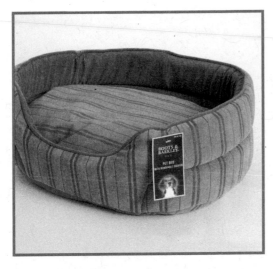

Skip It!

NONORGANIC PET BED

THE UGLY

Old pet beds with crumbling foam release flame retardants that can negatively affect your pet's health.

THE INCONVENIENT TRUTH

According to the World Health Organization (WHO), 20,000 deaths occur every year from pesticide poisoning in developing countries, many of which is from cotton farming.

Healthy Rx

If your pet is attached to an unhealthy bed, you can have a custom bed of natural wool or organic cotton made to fit the old cover.

PET DEODORIZER

Green It!

S.A.M ZER-ODOR™ REDUCER

THE GOOD
Zeolites are formed when volcanic rock and ash layers react with alkaline groundwater.

THE GREEN
S.A.M Zer-Odor Reducer is made of pure zeolites, natural volcanic minerals which absorb pungent odors. Easy to use and economical, simply sprinkle it beneath your pet's bedding or in a litter tray and the bag will last up to two months.

THE CONVENIENT TRUTH
Baking soda is inexpensive, removes odors rather than masking them, and is environmentally friendly, containing no harsh chemicals or irritating fragrances.

Ron's Green $$ Tip
Need a handy guide to take when pet shopping? Download this for free: www.petsfortheenviron ment.org/files/eddiestips.pdf.

Healthy Rx

As a natural deodorizer, baking soda can be sprinkled onto rugs and carpets and vacuumed after 10 to 15 minutes. Or mix the baking soda with a drop or two of essential oils or dried lavender before shaking onto carpet, and let sit for an hour or longer.

Skip It!

SCENTED PET DEODORIZER

THE UGLY

Don't opt to have your couches, carpets, and car upholstery treated with stain repellants—they're packed with toxic perfluorochemicals that can adversely affect your pet.

THE INCONVENIENT TRUTH

While powerfully scented carpet powders are capable of covering odors, they contain chemicals that your pet breathes in.

MOP

Green It!

METHOD® OMOP®

THE GOOD

Micro-manage your floor! Method omops come with a washable mop pad that has microfibers to help lift and trap dirt. They can be washed and reused up to 50 times, and the more you do so, the better they work as the microfibers split over time and therefore cover more ground when cleaning.

THE GREEN

Dust to dust . . . Sweeping your floor merely pushes the dust around. Method's corn-derived sweeping cloths catch the dust, and since they're compostable and biodegradable, you can simply toss the cloths in a compost bin when you are done. Even the box can be recycled like cardboard or also tossed into a compost bin.

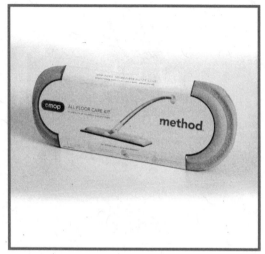

THE CONVENIENT TRUTH

Method omops are ergonomically shaped to minimize back strain as you mop.

Sage Advice

The Method omops are packaged with a nontoxic and biodegradable cleaner in yummy scents like lemon ginger or almond and packaged in a box created out of bamboo fiber and recycled paper.

Healthy Rx

You can lessen your pets' exposure to toxic chemicals in house dust simply by removing your shoes at the door.

Skip It!

NONBIODEGRADABLE MOP HEAD

THE UGLY

In the most comprehensive study of chemicals in pets, dogs were found to have 40% higher and cats to have 96% higher levels of chemicals than found in people. These chemicals include plasticizers, grease-proof chemicals, and fire retardants.

THE INCONVENIENT TRUTH

Every year, the U.S. goes through 83,000 tons of disposable wipes that generally end up in landfills. Worse yet, although traditional sweeper cloths feel like paper, they are actually made with plastic.

PET FOOD

Green It!

NEWMAN'S OWN® ORGANICS PREMIUM PET FOODS / PET PROMISE® DOG FOOD

THE GOOD

Newman's Own Organics pet food doesn't contain genetically modified organisms (GMOs). Over 70% of all ingredients are organic.

THE GREEN

Organic pet foods avoid wheat and corn, which can cause allergies in some pets. Organic pet food also means no chemical preservatives, no by-products, no added growth hormones and no antibiotic-fed protein.

THE CONVENIENT TRUTH

Not only will feeding your pet organic food decrease the amount of pesticides ingested, but it also supports

organic farming, which helps keep pesticides out of the soil and waterways.

Sage Advice

You can eliminate over 670 doses of artificial growth hormones administered to cattle, and 2,000 doses of antibiotics given to both chicken and cattle, simply by feeding your dog Pet Promise for a year!

Skip It!

NONORGANIC PET FOOD

THE UGLY

Just as you are what you eat, so are your pets. Unfortunately, most commercial pet foods contain rendered animal by-products.

THE INCONVENIENT TRUTH

In addition to byproducts, traditional pet foods are full of chemical additives, preservatives and dyes, all of which have been clinically linked to food allergies in both dogs and cats.

Sage Advice

Bodies of animals deemed unfit for consumption by the slaughterhouses, animals euthanized at shelters and vet's offices, expired meats and butcher trimmings, and even restaurant oils are all sent to rendering plants, where they are melted down into fatty grease—which is in turn used in pet foods!

DOG TOYS
Green It!

SIMPLYFIDO®
PET TOYS

THE GOOD
Simply Fido's adorable toys are offered in hemp and organic cotton, and are tested and certified 100% nontoxic.

THE GREEN
Simply Fido is dedicated to protecting the environment. Every Simply Fido collectible comes in a box hand crafted from recycled materials.

THE CONVENIENT TRUTH
Even the coloring of Simply Fido products is nontoxic, having originated from plants and minerals.

Sage Advice
The organic cotton used by SimplyFido is certified by the OCIA, the Organic Crop Improvement Association, which has been accredited by the USDA to certify products as organic since 1985.

Sage Advice
With their shorter life spans, pets develop health problems from such toxic exposures much more quickly.

Skip It!
PLASTIC DOG TOYS

THE UGLY
Most pet toys are made from materials including PVC. During production, they release dangerous dioxins into our air.

THE INCONVENIENT TRUTH
In the first study of its kind, the Environmental Working Group (EWG) found that pets absorb the pollutants in tap water, on lawns treated with pesticides, and in the air at higher levels than humans. Toxins used in plastic toys and medicines were discovered in tests of dogs that found that the animals were contaminated with breakdown products of four plastic softeners (phthalates) at higher levels than found in humans.

DOGGIE WASTE BAGS

Green It!

BIOBAG® DOG WASTE BAGS

THE GOOD
Mater-Bi, the material used to produce BioBags, is made from renewable raw materials including non-GMO starch, and is the first completely biodegradable and compostable bio-polymer ever invented.

THE GREEN
BioBag is made with GMO-free corn, contains no polyethylene, and was the first biodegradable and compostable "plastic" waste bag in the world.

THE CONVENIENT TRUTH
BioBags work great for kitchen and yard waste as well, and break down in approximately one month.

Sage Advice
Cat lovers can rejoice too, by avoiding non-biodegradable clay cat litter. Swheat Scoop® litter is made from naturally processed wheat, and World's Best Cat Litter is made from whole-kernel corn is flushable and septic safe. Both options are clay free, chemical free, and biodegradable.

Skip It!

NONBIODEGRADABLE CLEAN-UP BAGS

THE UGLY

Over 2 million tons of non-biodegradable cat litter made from clay ends up in municipal landfills each year. At the same time, 10 million tons of animal waste ends up in landfills, which can then seep into the ground and migrate into our drinking water.

THE INCONVENIENT TRUTH

Responsible owners pick up after their dog, but in doing so, put waste that is 100% biodegradable into plastic bags that can take more than 100 years to decompose.

If you wisely invest
in beauty, it will remain with
you all the days of your life.

FRANK LLOYD WRIGHT

CHAPTER 5

YOUR FAMILY:

BIG OR SMALL—
IDEAS FOR ALL

PRODUCE

Green It!

CLEAN 15:
ONION / AVOCADO /
SWEET CORN / PAPAYA /
PINEAPPLE / BROCCOLI
/MANGO / ASPARAGUS /
SWEET PEAS / TOMATO
/KIWI / WATER MELON
/CABBAGE / EGGPLANT /
SWEET POTATO

THE GOOD
These 15 fruits and vegetables contain the lowest pesticide residue. If budgeting, this means they are most likely the safest to buy conventional rather than organic.

THE GREEN
Buying organic is the only way to be sure your food is not saturated with pesticides.

THE CONVENIENT TRUTH
Typically, fruits and vegetables with a thicker skin (that is usually not consumed) contain less pesticide residue.

Lisa's D.I.Y.
Need a handy wallet guide to carry with you and make shopping easier?
Download it for free at www.foodnews.org.

Skip It!

**DIRTY DOZEN:
PEACH / APPLE / BELL
PEPPER / CELERY /
NECTARINE / CHERRIES /
STRAWBERRIES / KALE /
LETTUCE / GRAPES /
CARROT / PEAR**

THE UGLY

These 12 fruits and vegetable are consistently sprayed with pesticides and contain the highest amount of pesticide residues. Spend the extra money for the organic versions of these—your health is worth it.

- -

THE INCONVENIENT TRUTH

There was a time when the U.S. government said that DDT was safe. Don't wait for the government to catch up, take your health into your own hands and support organics.

- -

Mother Knows Best!

Produce has a PLU code on the sticker: Four digits are conventionally grown. Five digits beginning with "8" are GM (genetically engineered). Five digits starting with "9" are organically grown. There is an application for your iPhone available for download at foodnews.org/walletguide.php.

ENERGY DRINKS

Green It!

STEAZ® ENERGY DRINK

THE GOOD

Steaz Energy drink is Fair Trade certified, guaranteeing the farmers receive fair wages and safe working conditions.

THE GREEN

Steaz Energy drink uses organic ingredients, meaning they're grown without the use of pesticides, herbicides, fungicides, and fertilizers. They use caffeine that is naturally occurring in plants, rather than synthetic caffeine produced in a lab.

THE CONVENIENT TRUTH

Since their beginning, Steaz has donated over $100,000 to good causes such as the Sri Lanka Foundation, which supports the community where they source their tea and Grind for

Life, which provides financial aid to cancer patients and their families.

Sage Advice

Steaz is the official energy drink of The Green Energy Council. They have partnered with NativeEnergy in their efforts to promote the use of clean fuels and reduce their impact on the environment.

Healthy Rx

Drinking 1 cup of tea per day can provide your body with many health benefits and provide a natural caffeine boost without all the added sugar and artificial sweeteners found in many energy drinks.

Skip It!

NONORGANIC / NON-FAIR TRADE ENERGY DRINK

THE UGLY

Many energy drinks contain caffeine from concentrated plant extracts or synthetic caffeine as opposed to a naturally occurring source.

THE INCONVENIENT TRUTH

Over 3 *billion* cans of Red Bull were sold in more than 130 countries—and that was just in the year 2006 alone!

Red Bull is more expensive than other, more natural sources of caffeine.

CARBONATED BEVERAGES

Green It!

IZZE®

THE GOOD

Sparkling juices like IZZE and organic teas are a healthy alternative to diet sodas, providing a low-calorie refreshing source for the body.

THE GREEN

Tea is one of the fourteen so-called SuperFoods. Drinking one cup a day can help prevent cancer and osteoporosis. Tea also has natural anti-viral and anti-inflammatory properties.

THE CONVENIENT TRUTH

If you choose to drink diet soda, choose a natural one such as Blue Sky Lite (made with real sugar) or Zevia Natural Soda sweetened with stevia.

Sage Advice

Want to reduce your soda intake? Try sparkling water, club soda, or seltzer. These will provide the same satisfaction as a carbonated beverage without all the artificial ingredients and sugar. Try all three as they each have their own distinct flavor.

Skip It!

DIET SODA W/ ARTIFICIAL SWEETENER

THE UGLY

Diet sodas contain artificial sweeteners that offer no benefit to the body and may actually cause health issues. These artificial sweeteners include aspartame (NutraSweet), sucralose (Splenda), acesulfame, potassium, saccharine, and high fructose corn syrup.

THE INCONVENIENT TRUTH

Beware of the "As!" Aspartame is also found in both diet food and sodas. Acesulfame-K is a newer sweetener, which can be found in soft drinks and some baked goods.

Sage Advice

The phosphoric acid in soda leaches calcium from our bones and can lead to osteoporosis.

SWEETENERS

Green It!

STEVIA® / 100% ORGANIC AGAVE NECTAR

THE GOOD
Stevia has been used as a sweetener for centuries in Paraguay, and agave has been used in Mexico for centuries.

THE GREEN
Stevia and agave nectar are plant derived sweeteners and do not contain any artificial or harmful chemicals.

THE CONVENIENT TRUTH
Stevia and agave nectar are absorbed slowly into the blood stream, so they won't cause a spike in blood sugar or insulin levels, making them ideal for diabetics or for anyone trying to control their weight.

Sage Advice

Need another reason to use natural sweeteners? Wastewater carries some unnatural additives, namely artificial sweeteners that could be finding their way into your drinking water. Even after having gone through sewage treatment, artificial sweeteners have been found in wastewater according to researchers at the Water Technology Center in Germany.

Skip It!

ARTIFICIAL SWEETENER

THE UGLY

The sweetening agent in Sweet'N Low is saccharin, which has been linked to bladder cancer. Splenda (sucralose) is a chlorocarbon and Equal (aspartame) is an excitotoxin. These are three chemicals that offer absolutely no health benefit to the body and over time will potentially lead to health problems.

THE INCONVENIENT TRUTH

Chlorocarbons are not compatible with the human metabolism. They are known to cause genetic and reproductive damage.

Healthy Rx

Make an effort to read labels and avoid artificial sweeteners. Brain tumors and lymphoma in rodents have been linked to consumption of high amounts of the sweetener according to some research.

MILK

Green It!

STONEYFIELD FARM®
ORGANIC MILK /
ORGANIC YOGURT

THE GOOD

Stoneyfield Farms products consist of natural and organic ingredients while avoiding preservatives, artificial flavors, colors, and sweeteners. The ingredients are produced without the use of antibiotics, artificial growth hormones, chemical fertilizers, and toxic and persistent pesticides. Or try Organic Valley, which has been farmer owned since 1988. Today, the largest organic farming cooperative in the U.S. has grown to include 1326 organic farmers who support their local communities.

THE GREEN

Organic farmers practice humane treatment of animals and the farming methods respect the Earth and nurture animals.

THE CONVENIENT TRUTH

Hungry for change? The makers of the 2009 movie *Food, Inc.* "lift the veil on our nation's food industry, exposing the highly mechanized underbelly that has been hidden from the American consumer with the consent of our government's regulatory agencies, USDA and FDA." Learn more: www.foodincmovie .com.

Mother Knows Best!
You are what you eat: USDA organic food produced without antibiotics, added growth hormones, or pesticides means a healthier you and a happier planet.

Skip It!

NONORGANIC / GMO DAIRY

THE UGLY
Dairy cows from non-organic farms are often injected with growth hormones such as rBGH/rBST to increase milk production.

Genetically engineered bovine growth hormone (rBGH/rBST) has been linked to breast, colon, and prostate cancers.

IGF-1 in rBGH milk may cause breast enlargement in children and infants.

THE INCONVENIENT TRUTH
European nations and Canada have put a ban on rBGH in order to protect their citizens. Meanwhile, the FDA allows genetically modified rBGH to be added to U.S. milk. American made cheese will contain rBGH/rBST unless otherwise stated. Cheeses imported from Europe are safer to eat.

NON DAIRY

Green It!

PACIFIC® ORGANIC ALMOND AND OAT MILKS / 365® ORGANIC RICEMILK / LIGHTLIFE® ORGANIC TEMPEH

THE GOOD

Stick with soy foods that are fermented and organic soy products such as Tempeh, Miso, and Natto. Always look for "non-GMO" on the label. Defined as "genetically modified organism," GMO refers to a living organism whereby a gene from an unrelated species is inserted into the organism to alter the original gene. It is also referred to as "transgenic" technology.

THE GREEN

Replace your tofu with tempeh. Replace your soy milk with nut milk or hemp milk. If you use protein powder, stick with whey or egg whites or a vegetarian formula that does not contain soy.

THE CONVENIENT TRUTH

According to the National Agricultural Statistics Service, soybean crops' area was estimated at a record high 77.5 million acres for 2009. That is second to corn at 87 million acres.

Sage Advice

Genetically modified crops, particularly corn and soybeans, are popular with U.S. farmers. St. Louis-based Monsanto is the leading developer of such crops.

Skip It!
TOFU / SOY MILK

THE UGLY
Tofu and soy milk are unfermented soy products which can have a negative impact on thyroid function. Some studies show that infant formulas made with soy cause an increased risk in autoimmune thyroid disease in children and an increased risk in thyroid cancer.

THE INCONVENIENT TRUTH
Soy contains anti-nutrients that block digestive enzymes and is high in plant estrogens. Today, over 80% of U.S. corn, soybean and cotton crops are genetically modified. Two dozen countries, including the U.S. allow the cultivation of biotech crops, while much of Europe, Japan, and most of Africa remain opposed to genetically altered crops.

Mother Knows Best!
Excess estrogen in men can cause a "spare tire" and "man boobs." Soy has been touted as a "health food" and unrightfully so. Many groups of people should avoid soy products due do its high phytoestrogen (plant estrogens) content. These groups include women with a history or family history of breast cancer, and post-menopausal women and men.

COOKIES

Green It!

NEWMAN'S OWN ORGANICS® NEWMAN-O'S

THE GOOD

Newman's Own Organics assures consumers that its producers take measures to certify that all of the cocoa it purchases is produced without the use of forced labor.

THE GREEN

Paul Newman and Newman's Own Foundation have given over $265 million to thousands of charities worldwide since 1982. The Newman's Own Organics product ingredients are grown on farms that have not used artificial fertilizers or pesticides for three years or more. Its products are certified organic by Oregon Tilth and are also Kosher certified.

THE CONVENIENT TRUTH

Newman-O's uses clean ingredients like organic sugar, are free of partially hydrogenated oils and do not contain trans-fatty acids.

Sage Advice

Flavors abound! Don't like the filling? No problem. These healthy O's are also available in Peanut Butter Crème Filled Chocolate Cookies, Mint Crème, Crème Filled Ginger Cookies, and Wheat Free, Dairy Free Crème.

Skip It!
NONORGANIC COOKIES

THE UGLY
Oreos contain high fructose corn syrup, enriched (highly processed) flour, and artificial flavors. While most chocolate chip cookies contain butter and hydrogenated oils, Newman's Champion Chip Cookies remove non-organic, conventional butter, and replace it with an organic palm fruit oil which contains no hydrogenated oils.

- -

THE INCONVENIENT TRUTH
Many cookies are cheaper than Newman-O's, but they are also made with cheaper, less nutritious ingredients.

- -

Sage Advice
Newman's Own cooperatives are inspected to verify compliance with organic standards. They require written verification from the inspector that each farm is "slavery free."

NUT SPREADS

Green It!

ALMOND BUTTER / SUNFLOWER SEED SPREAD

THE GOOD

Nut butters are an excellent source of protein and are cholesterol free. Almond butter is rich in monounsaturated fat (a good fat).

THE GREEN

Manitoba Harvest Hemp Seed Butter contains no trans fats, hydrogenated oils, cholesterol, added sugar, gluten, preservatives, artificial colors, or artificial flavors and is low in saturated fat. A farmer-owned company, they operate a 100% wind powered, organic, and kosher-certified facility.

THE CONVENIENT TRUTH

A good brand of nut butter will not contain trans fats, hydrogenated oils, or preservatives. It should only contain nuts and sometimes salt. There is no need to add sugar or oil as nuts contain natural oils.

Sage Advice

Hemp seeds contain all the essential amino acids needed by the human body, and are a balanced source of Omega-3 and Omega-6 Essential Fatty Acids (EFAs).

Healthy Rx

Switching out your conventional peanut butter for nut butter such as almond butter or hemp seed butter is the difference between junk food and health food. Manitoba Harvest Hemp Seed Butter is made from shelled hemp seed that is grown sustainably, without herbicides or pesticides, and contains no GMOs.

Skip It!

HYDROGENATED OIL / SUGAR-CONTAINING PEANUT SPREADS

THE UGLY

Jif's reduced-fat peanut butter contains corn syrup solids, sugar, and soy, along with the hydrogenated oils. Even Jif's "Natural" peanut butter contains unnecessary oil and sugar.

THE INCONVENIENT TRUTH

Most brand name peanut butters contain sugar and partially hydrogenated and hydrogenated oils.

WINE

Green It!

ORGANIC WINE

THE GOOD

In a European study of six different organic wines, five of the wines tested contained no detectable pesticide residues, providing further validation that pesticide-free wine production is possible.

THE GREEN

Used by some vineyards, such as America's first organic winery, Frey Vineyards, biodynamic agriculture is a method of organic farming that is guided by the seasons and treats the farms as a unified solid organism. Frey wines contain no added sulfites (a synthetic food additive).

THE CONVENIENT TRUTH

Bonterra vineyards in California were one of the first major vineyards to commit to organic and sustainable

wine growing. New to the Sterling collection are wines "made with organic grapes," which indicates that grapes are free from artificial fertilizers and synthetic chemicals consisting of a Chardonnay (2007), Sauvignon Blanc (2007), and Cabernet Sauvignon (2009).

Sage Advice

Two-thirds of all global wine production and consumption is from Europe.

Skip It!

NONORGANIC WINES

THE UGLY

In 2008 Pesticide Action Network (PAN) Europe tested wines made by world famous vineyards and discovered that each wine sampled contained an average of at least four pesticides. One bottle actually contained ten known pesticides!

THE INCONVENIENT TRUTH

In general, grapes receive higher doses of synthetic pesticides than virtually any other type of crop in Europe. This should concern Americans because the U.S. is currently second in the world for total amount of global wine consumption.

Healthy Rx

According to the Environmental Working Group, a published PAN-Europe report suggests the health impacts of pesticide exposure to vineyard farm workers are a concern. It showed that farmers had higher incidence of allergic rhinitis, respiratory problems, cancers, and other health effects.

SPIRITS
Green It!
ORGANIC VODKA

THE GOOD
Rye and wheat are the classic grains for making vodka. However, for a unique organic vodka, try Prairie Organic Vodka, which is distilled from corn.

THE GREEN
VeeV, the wheat-based (but *not* certified organic) vodka, is infused with 100% all-natural ingredients including Acai and is a certified carbon-neutral company. And it donates $1 per bottle sold to the Brazilian rain forest.

Distilled from certified organic rye, Square One Organic Vodka boosts a very green packaging process. The face label of the bottle is made from bamboo, bagasse (sugar cane pulp), and cotton, and they are packed in chlorine-free shipper cartons.

THE CONVENIENT TRUTH
Vodka is created by fermenting and then distilling the simple sugars from a mash of pale grain or vegetal matter.

Mother Knows Best!
Due to its alcohol content there are numerous recipes utilizing vodka from cleaning jewelry or making insect repellant spray to scrubbing away bathroom mildew.

Skip It!

UNSUSTAINABLE OR NONORGANIC VODKA

THE UGLY
Too much of a good thing: In one study, it was reported that low to moderate alcohol consumption (8 to 14 drinks per week) was detrimental to brain health and actually caused brain shrinkage.

THE INCONVENIENT TRUTH
Chances are that if a company is not advertising its green business practices, it is not very green.

Sage Advice
It is a higher carbon footprint to drink imported vodka.

WATER

Green It!

KLEAN KANTEEN™ / THINK SPORT® / THERMOS STAINLESS STEEL INTAK® HYDRATION BOTTLE

THE GOOD
Kleen Kanteens are food grade stainless steel and BPA free.

THE GREEN
Reusing safe water containers eliminates plastic water bottles which crowd our landfills and tax our energy resources. Made from PET (a petroleum product), and utilizing oil (a nonrenewable resource) plastic bottle production leads to increased CO_2 emissions. If that doesn't convince you—they create trash and can harm your health by leaching chemicals into water.

THE CONVENIENT TRUTH
Want to save 1.5 million barrels of oil consumption and about 38 billion water bottles from ending up in landfills each year? According to Britta's Filter for Good campaign, Americans can do this just by avoiding bottled water.

Mother Knows Best!

Read between the lines! If the small print on your bottled water reads "from a municipal source" or "from a community water system" its source is likely the same as your tap water.

Skip It!
BOTTLED WATER

THE UGLY

According to the Clean Air Council, *Americans throw away 2.5 million plastic bottles every hour.* Didn't get your attention? The Container Recycling Institute states only 14% of them are recycled.

THE INCONVENIENT TRUTH

Plastic water bottles end up as litter on our landscape, taking up to 1,000 years to biodegrade.

With over 1,000 individual tests performed on more than 100 brands of bottled water, it has been determined that bottled water was not necessarily any purer than most tap water. Some bottled water was actually very high in quality and purity, though other brands contained elevated levels of bacteria, arsenic, and other contaminants.

COFFEE
Green It!

GREEN MOUNTAIN® ROASTERS / 365® WHOLE FOODS / NEWMAN'S OWN® ORGANIC

THE GOOD

Teeccino, a popular coffee substitute, is actually roasted and ground to brew and taste just like coffee. It is naturally caffeine free, contains no chemical residue, and provides a natural energy boost from nutrients versus stimulants like caffeine.

THE GREEN

If you drink coffee, only drink organic and fair-trade brands. Organic coffee beans are grown without toxic pesticides or chemical fertilizers. Fair trade organizations provide farmers with stable prices that help them to have a reasonable standard of living.

THE CONVENIENT TRUTH

With the availability of coffee in the U.S., it is no wonder the average American adult consumes more than 10 pounds of coffee per year.
 Most major decaf coffee brands are chemically decaffeinated.

Sage Advice

"Decaf" coffee still contains caffeine. If you are going to drink decaffeinated coffee, try "Swiss Water Process" decaf. It has a 100% chemical-free process that results in 99.9% caffeine free.

Mother Knows Best!
When brewing your own organic coffee or Teeccino, only use unbleached coffee filters. Many generic coffee filters have chlorine bleach in them, which may be leached from the filter into the coffee .

Skip It!
NONORGANIC COFFEE

THE UGLY
Too much caffeine can over stimulate the adrenal glands, causing symptoms of fatigue, insomnia, mood swings, and weight gain. It can even suppress the immune system.

THE INCONVENIENT TRUTH
Coffee is a heavily sprayed crop, and is usually not grown in the U.S.; therefore, we don't have much control over how much pesticide the coffee is being treated with. Unfortunately, pesticides have been linked to health problems like Parkinson's Disease, miscarriages in pregnant women, and prostate and other cancers.

SEAFOOD

Green It!

LOBSTER / WILD ALASKAN SALMON / FARM-RAISED BAY SCALLOPS

THE GOOD
Fish is an excellent source of protein that is low in fat and is high in omega-3 fatty acids, the "good" fats.

THE GREEN
Download the Environmental Defense Fund's Pocket Seafood Selector to find healthier choices of seafood at www.edf.org/page.cfm?tagID=1521.

THE CONVENIENT TRUTH
Wild Alaskan salmon, sardines, and farmed rainbow trout are all great examples of seafood that are lower in environmental contaminants, but high in healthy omega 3s. Visit montereybayaquarium.org to download a guide.

OCEAN-FRIENDLY FISH

Farmed: Arctic Char, Barramundi, Catfish, Clams, Mussels, Oysters, Bay Scallops, Sturgeon, Caviar, Tilapia, Rainbow Trout, Albacore Tuna, Spiny Lobster
Wild: Cod (Alaska longline), Dungeness & Stone Crab, Halibut (Pacific), Pollock (Alaska), Lobster, Salmon (Alaska), Skipjack Tuna

Skip It!

NON-OCEAN FRIENDLY SEAFOOD

THE UGLY
Despite many health benefits, eating fish that are contaminated with toxins and chemicals can pose considerable health risks in the long run. Some fish are high in mercury, lead, and even pesticides. Find out at NRDC.org.

THE INCONVENIENT TRUTH
Many fish are disappearing from the oceans because the ocean ecosystem isn't doing well.

According to the Environmental Defense Fund, grouper is the worst fish to eat. Not only do grouper tend to have elevated levels of mercury, many species of grouper are being over-harvested from their environment.

NON OCEAN-FRIENDLY FISH

Imported: King Crab, Spiny Lobster (Caribbean), Mahi mahi/ Dolphinfish, Caviar, Swordfish, Yellowtail (Australia or Japan, farmed)
Domestic: Chilean Seabass/ Toothfish, Cod (Atlantic), Flounders, Soles (Atlantic), Groupers, Halibut (Atlantic), Blue Marlin, Striped Monkfish, Orange Roughy, Rockfish (Pacific trawled), Salmon (farmed, including Atlantic), Sharks, Shrimp (imported farmed or wild), Red Snapper, Sturgeon, Albacore Tuna (wild), Bigeye, Yellowfin (longline), Bluefin Tuna

CONVENIENCE OVENS

Green It!

GLOBAL SUN OVEN®

THE GOOD

The Global Sun Oven is called an oven, but food can be baked, boiled, steamed, and roasted at cooking temperatures of 360°F / 182°C. The initial price of a Global Sun Oven might be higher, but due to its long life (20+ years), its number of unique features, its ability to cook on partly cloudy days, and ability to keep food warm for hours, it offers a lot of value. Check out sunoven.com/index.php for more information on the product.

resources but live in sun-rich areas.

THE GREEN

Solar cookers reduce fuel needs by a third. Visit Solar Cookers World Network for more information.

THE CONVENIENT TRUTH

Sun ovens are the logical choice for the 1 billion people who have scarce wood

Sage Advice

Solar cookers are saving the lives of two million families who live in fuel-starved, sun-rich areas across the world. They help millions more to improve the health, economies and environments of some very impoverished regions.

Present day solar food technologies are not only clean, safe, convenient, and pollution free; they also help to reduce intestinal and respiratory diseases.

Skip It!

MICROWAVE

THE UGLY

In 1976 the Soviet Union banned the use of microwave ovens after a series of studies concluded they were harmful for human use.

THE INCONVENIENT TRUTH

Say no to microwaves! A Russian microwave-food science study discovered carcinogenic compounds were formed in virtually all foods that were tested. The study included foods like thawed frozen fruit, prepared meats, and frozen vegetables, and all were subject to normal microwave cooking conditions. For more information on the study go to www.healbuildings .com.

Sage Advice

Percy LeBaron Spencer of the Raytheon Company accidentally discovered the use of microwave energy. After realizing a melted candy bar in his pocket was the result of radar waves, the link to cooking food fast was found.

Microwave ovens are in 90% of America's homes.

TV
Green It!
LCD TV

THE GOOD

Go with LCD over plasma. The smaller LCD screen models use less energy and contain fewer hazardous chemicals than larger plasma screens.

THE GREEN

Properly recycling your television helps prevent toxins like lead and cadmium from getting into our landfills and eventually into our ecosystem. Look for community recycling events or local drop-off stations in your area that will recycle and reuse salvageable materials.

THE CONVENIENT TRUTH

Older Cathode ray tube (CRT) television sets actually uses less energy than either a plasma or LCD set.

Ron's Green $$ Tip

Smaller LCD screen televisions (less than 27 inches) can be more cost effective to operate than larger plasma models because they use less energy. LCDs also tend to have a much longer life span than plasma, giving you more value for your money.

Skip It!

PLASMA TV

THE UGLY

Little attention is focused on where recycled electronics end up. Of those televisions that are recycled, half end up overseas in poorer regions of the world where they are worked on (stripped for parts and metals) by impoverished families and children, who expose themselves to hazardous substances left over from the disposed television sets.

THE INCONVENIENT TRUTH

PBDEs (Polybrominated diphenylethers) are chemicals used as fire retardants in the plastics of TVs (both LCD and plasma) that can accumulate in people and ultimately disrupt hormone systems and even brain development.

Sage Advice

Beware of screen burn. Plasma televisions have been known to generate excessive heat, which can cause permanent disfigurement of areas on the screen.

PHONES

Green It!

900 MHZ
CORDLESS PHONE /
CORDED PHONE

THE GOOD

A 900 MHz cordless phone gives off a weaker electrical pulse than higher 2.5 and 5.8 GHz phones and is the healthier choice for your home.

THE GREEN

You can help go greener by not using the phone book. When you go to www.yellowpagesgoesgreen.org you can stop the delivery of unsolicited telephone books being sent to your house.

THE CONVENIENT TRUTH

You can test your home for Electromagnetic Pollution. Consult with a Building Biology Environmental Consultant (BBEC) near you and learn how to create a healthier living environ-

ment for you and your family. As part of a BBECs testing protocol, radio frequency risk assessments can be conducted on the effect of your current digital cordless phones and other wireless devices that may be affecting your living space. Check out buildingbiology.net for a consultant near you.

Healthy Rx

Best to avoid cordless and excess wireless exposure all together—especially in sleeping areas. In addition, when you opt for non-wireless phones that don't require a power source, they will still work even during a power outage.

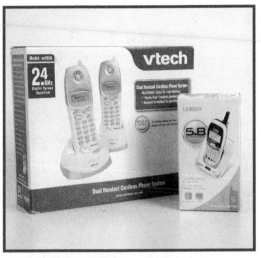

THE INCONVENIENT TRUTH

Can't sleep? Try removing all cordless phones away from the head of your bed (and out of your room all together. This is true of phones that are adjacent to your bedroom walls from other rooms as well. Studies are revealing that the digital communication of these phones and other wireless devices can be disrupting your sleep and affecting your health.

Skip It!

2.4 GHZ CORDLESS PHONE / 5.8 GHZ CORDLESS PHONE

THE UGLY

Research has shown that digital communications from technology like 2.5 and 5.8 GHz cordless phones can be detrimental to your health. In fact, some specialist doctors working with parents of autistic children and those exhibiting motor neuron disease (such as Alzheimer's) are now convinced that this type of digital pollution accelerates brain deterioration by destruction of brain synapses.

Healthy Rx

Avoid wireless when you can. A BBEC can provide mitigation techniques to help reduce your exposure to electromagnetic radiation in your home in areas that you may not be aware of.

DEODORANT

Green It!

NATURALLY FRESH CRYSTAL SPRAY MIST / SOLAY® SALT STONE / LĀFE'S® NATURAL DEODORANT SPRAY

THE GOOD

Crystal Body deodorant products are 100% hypoallergenic and are fragrance, chemical, and paraben free. They are all-natural mineral salt deodorants containing no aluminum chloride or alcohol and are stain resistant.

THE GREEN

Direct from nature, the salt stone has natural deodorant properties through its ability to disinfect and neutralize odors. It naturally prevents the formation of germs and bacteria that cause unpleasant body odor.

THE CONVENIENT TRUTH

Each square inch of your skin contains

95 to 100 oil glands and 650 sweat glands. Choose roll on or pump spray instead of using aerosol products. Not only can they be respiratory irritants.

Ron's Green $$ Tip

Make your own! Even some trusted names include toxic ingredients according to EWG's Skin Deep database. Rest assured you can make reliable and affordable deodorants using a homemade recipe: Combine baking soda (to deodorize) and cornstarch (to deodorize and absorb moisture) together and apply to damp skin!

Skip It!

ANTIPERSPIRANT / DEODORANT WITH CHEMICALS OR ALUMINUM

THE UGLY

National Geographic's online resource, The Green Guide, has a list called 'The Dirty Dozen.' Of these 12 products to avoid, 6 can be found in deodorants: antibacterials, dieth-anolamine (DEA), formaldehyde, petroleum distillates, fragrance, and parabens.

THE INCONVENIENT TRUTH

Conventional deodorants reduce sweat and odor-producing bacteria by shrinking pores which inhibits the body from excreting toxins. They often contain chemicals such as: alcohol, aluminum, zinc, silica, talc, and other byproducts that can contain hormone disruptors, chemicals linked to cancer. Even the healthy versions mask odor with fragrance and can cause skin irritation.

Sage Advice

Companies are not required by the FDA to test their own products for safety before placing them on store shelves. Loopholes allow manufactures to put almost any product they want into personal care products including lead, mercury, placenta, fragrance, nanoparticles, phthlates, animal parts, petroleum by-products, and more.

TOOTHPASTE
Green It!

TRADER JOE'S® / TOM'S OF MAINE® / PEELU®

THE GOOD
Look for brands of toothpaste that don't contain fluoride, saccharin, or other known toxic ingredients. Sodium Lauryl Sulfate (SLS) is found in highly rated brands, but avoiding it when possible is advised.

THE GREEN
The biggest environmental impact of toothpaste usually comes from its ingredients. Choosing natural ingredients can make a difference to our ecosystem. Also look for xylitol, a natural sugar found effective in preventing tooth decay.

THE CONVENIENT TRUTH
Stevia is a natural sweetener that is used as a healthy alternative to Saccharin in toothpaste.

Sage Advice
In the cleaning industry, Sodium Lauryl Sulfate (SLS) is used to clean garage floors. SLS is a drying agent which has a foaming effect that can be found in some toothpaste, but is also used for cleaning things like grease off garage floors. Look for options like Tom's of Main SLS-free toothpastes which use glycyrrhizin, derived from licorice root, to foam and disperse ingredients.

Skip It!

FLUORIDE / ARTIFICIAL SWEETENER OR SLS-CONTAINING TOOTHPASTE

THE UGLY

Fluoride can be deadly in large doses and there is enough fluoride in typical tube of toothpaste to kill a small child if ingested. According to the *Journal of Dental Research*, the Probably Toxic Dose (PTD) for fluoride is 5mg/kg. If a child ingests a fluoride dose in excess of 15mg/kg, then death is likely to occur. It can be fatal for some children even at doses as low as 5 mg/kg.

THE INCONVENIENT TRUTH

Wholesale shipments of toothpaste go even a step further and must have the poison symbol of skull and cross-bones on the container.

Sage Advice

The addition of fluoride to toothpaste prompted manufacturers in the U.S. to have warning labels required by the FDA stating: "WARNING: Keep out of reach of children under 6 years of age. If you accidentally swallow more than used for brushing, seek professional help or contact a poison control center immediately."

FOUNDATION / POWDER

Green It!
REJUVA® MINERALS / COASTAL CLASSIC CREATIONS® / JANE IREDALE® / ZOSIMOS® BOTANICALS

THE GOOD
You can choose to eliminate the use of chemicals linked to cancer, birth defects, and other health problems by joining the campaign for safe cosmetics at www.safecosmetics.org.

THE GREEN
Choose foundations free of the Green Guide's (the greenguide.com) "Dirty Dozen" chemicals like antibacterials, coal-tar dyes, 1,4-dioxane, formaldehyde, fragrance, mercury, nanoparticles, and petroleum distillates. Incorporate certified organic antioxidants instead.

THE CONVENIENT TRUTH
Check the Skin Deep database to see how your current makeup rates against thousands tested at www.cosmeticsdatabase.com/index.php.

Sage Advice
Emmy-winner Jane Iredale was the first to introduce mineral makeup to the industry. Her makeup line will not block pores, includes UVB and UVA protection, is anti-inflammatory, contains no talc, parabens, or nano particle sizes, and is not tested on animals.

Sage Advice

Crushed beetles in your makeup? Yes, if you see "carmine" on the ingredients. The dye is made from these little creatures.

Skip It!
CHEMICAL-LADEN MAKEUP

THE UGLY

Be sure to focus on the ingredients in all of your personal care products, because current laws don't require manufacturers to substantiate their marketing claims. Don't trust any terms like *natural* and *hypoallergenic*, as they are not regulated.

THE INCONVENIENT TRUTH

Many ingredients found in generic foundations are linked to cancer, reproductive toxicity, allergies, irritation (skin, eyes, or lungs), enhanced skin absorption, and biochemical, and cellular level changes.

SHAVING CREAM

Green It!

DR. BRONNER'S MAGIC ALL-ONE® / TOM'S OF MAINE® / AUBREY® ORGANICS

THE GOOD

It is always safer to choose fragrance free or unscented shaving creams and gels if you cannot verify where the scent is derived from.

THE GREEN

Look for shaving gels that do not contain triclosan, which can accumulate in the environment and is hazardous to aquatic life.

THE CONVENIENT TRUTH

Dr. Bronner's shave gels are Certified Fair Trade, USDA organic, and not tested on animals. Aubrey Organics are vegan and not tested on animals. Tom's of Maine products do not test on or contain animal products, artificial colors, flavors, scents, preservatives, ethylene glycol, parabens, peroxide, phthalates, artificial sweeteners, or triclosan.

Sage Advice

When substances are applied to the skin, they get absorbed into the bloodstream. Many health food stores have healthier options of shaving gels and creams to choose from.

Skip It!
ARTIFICIALLY SCENTED SHAVING CREAM WITH PRESEVERATIVE

THE UGLY
More than one-third of all personal care products by third party testing contains at least one ingredient linked to cancer.

Phthalates are often a part of the blend of chemicals that are hidden under products ingredients listed as "fragrance." Phthalates have been linked to health concerns such as birth defects, developmental problems, and in extreme cases, cancer.

THE INCONVENIENT TRUTH
Of people who are exposed to fragrance, 20% experience health problems. It is estimated that the percentage of people allergic to chemicals will increase to 60% by the year 2020.

Sage Advice
The Organic Consumers Association's "Coming Clean Campaign" is dedicated to organic integrity in the labeling of personal care products after 2008 testing revealed many companies claiming to be organic were falsely labeled as such. OCA has been working to clean up the "natural" and "organic" personal care industry for the past five years. If you don't see the USDA Organic Seal, then chances are it's not totally organic.

MOUTHWASH

Green It!

TOM'S OF MAINE® / JÄSŌN® HEALTHY MOUTH

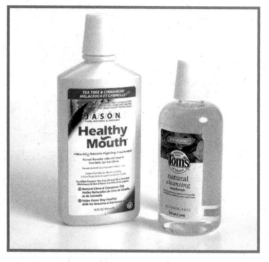

THE GOOD

Look for alcohol-free mouthwashes like Jason, Miessence and Tom's of Maine brands which are saccharin free and alcohol free. According to the National Cancer Institute, mouthwash with over 25% alcohol lead to higher risks of oral and throat cancer in men by 60%, and women up to 90%.

THE GREEN

As a result of the Tom's of Maine company using recycled cartons, they saved an estimated 376,396 pounds of solid waste in 2005.

THE CONVENIENT TRUTH

Chewing fresh parsley can actually sweeten your breath.

Sage Advice

Some mouthwashes only provide temporary relief from bad breath and fail to kill the bacteria source that is responsible for the problem.

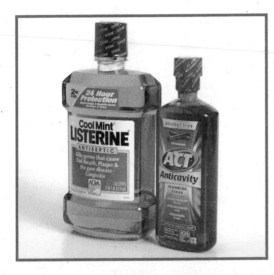

Skip It!

ALCOHOL BASED / ARTIFICIALLY SWEETENED MOUTHWASH

THE UGLY

Conventional mouthwashes commonly contain many unfriendly ingredients like alcohol, coal-tar colorants, formaldehyde, synthetic sweeteners, flavoring, and many other toxic concoctions.

THE INCONVENIENT TRUTH

Formaldehyde has a long list of adverse health effects and if ingested can cause severe physical reactions like internal bleeding, coma, and even death.

Sage Advice

Many name brand mouthwashes are manufactured with toxic dyes, chemical additives, synthetic sweeteners, and antimicrobial agents. These chemicals are not only bad for us, but they can get into our water supply and can wreak havoc to the environment.

FRAGRANCE

Green It!

TRILLIUM ORGANICS® / MOUNTAIN GIRL BOTANICS®

THE GOOD
Make healthier decisions by being aware of hidden ingredients that mask synthetic fragrances. Manufacturers are protected by their trade secrets, so one fragrance could be made up of hundreds of different chemicals.

THE GREEN
Scents that have very few ingredients and labeled with terms "USDA Organic" or "wildcrafted" are helpful indicators that can assist you in identifying if the product is organic.

THE CONVENIENT TRUTH
Choose 100% essential-oil fragranced perfumes and colognes; most are free of contaminants like phthalates.

Sage Advice
Beware of marketing terms including "unscented," "fragrance free," "no perfumes, dyes, or additives," "hypoallergenic," and "cruelty free and organic." If they are not certified, then they may not mean anything whatsoever.

Skip It!

ARTIFICIALLY FRAGRANCED PERFUME

THE UGLY

More than 95% of the chemicals used in fragrances are neurotoxic and derived from petroleum. They have been known to be harmful to the brain and nervous system.

THE INCONVENIENT TRUTH

The term "fragrance," "fragrance oil," "perfume oil," or "parfum" may be masking the presence of phthalates which are often used to disperse fragrance in perfumes. Linked to thyroid and reproductive disorders, they may be listed as DBP (di-n-butyl phthalate) or DEP (diethyl phthalate) on the ingredients label.

Sage Advice

The EPA found the following health problems associated with fragrance exposure: asthma, fatigue, eye irritation, sinusitis, skin problems, kidney and liver damage, immune system damage, nausea, blood pressure change (drop or rise), cancer, and even death due to respiratory failure.

SHAMPOO

Green It!

SOLAY® UNSCENTED GREEN TEA SHAMPOO / MGA® SHAMPOO

THE GOOD
Max Green Alchemy uses ingredients that are of 100% plant origin in their products. They are also free of animal-derived ingredients (Certified Vegan by Vegan Action) and animal testing (Certified Cruelty Free by the Coalition for Consumer Information on Cosmetics).

THE GREEN
Healing Scents uses organically grown ingredients, cold-processed oils, and therapeutic-grade essential oils. Like the other *Green This* shampoos, they don't contain any petroleum-based chemicals, like coal tar.

THE CONVENIENT TRUTH
The Solay Shine shampoos are made by hand in small batches, insuring freshness and quality. No fragrances, preservatives, or parabens are used.

Lisa's D.I.Y.
For fighting dandruff: after shampooing, rinse with a solution of ½ cup white vinegar and 2 cups of warm water.

For moisturizing your hair: make a hair mask. Just add equal parts conditioner and olive oil. Gently massage the mix into your hair; wrap it in a hot towel for 15 minutes, then rinse.

Sage Advice

For more information on what ingredients are in your shampoo, check out the Skin Deep cosmetic safety database at www.ewg.org/skindeep.

Skip It!

SYNTHETIC FRAGRANCE OR CHEMICAL-LADEN SHAMPOO

THE UGLY

A petrochemical waste called coal tar is an active ingredient in some dandruff shampoos and anti-itch creams. Avoid these when listed on the ingredients: FD&C Blue 1 and FD&C Green 3 found to be carcinogenic in animal studies.

THE INCONVENIENT TRUTH

Avoid shampoo ingredients such as 1,4 dioxane, diethanolamine (DEA), formaldehyde, parabens, sodium lauryl sulfate, sodium laureth sulfate, synthetic fragrances, and phthalates.

DEA is a wetting agent used in shampoos to create thick lather. Avoid it and other similar chemicals such as monoethanolamine (MEA) and triethanolamine (TEA).

FACIAL CLEANSER

Green It!

NATURE'S PLUS® NATURAL BEAUTY CLEANSING BAR / CVS® FACIAL CLEANSING PADS

THE GOOD
Using natural facial cleansers instead of soap is a better choice for your skin, as milder cleansers don't remove your skin's own natural oils.

THE GREEN
The Nature's Plus Natural Beauty Cleansing Bar is a great example of a cleanser that is not made of soap.

THE CONVENIENT TRUTH
Sodium Laureth Sulphate (SLES) and Ammonium Lauryl Sulfate (ALS) are commonly used in shampoos and cleansers. They are milder foaming agents than SLS, but linked to skin irritation. Instead, look for Sodium Lauryl Sulphoacetate (SLSA) instead derived from coconut and palm oils.

Sage Advice
Less is more! According to EWG, women on average use 12 products a day and 170 distinctive chemicals. Try to reduce your exposure to toxins by limiting the number of personal products incorporated into your daily routine.

Sage Advice

The Jäson satin soap, although a trusted name, contains fragrance and benzyl alcohol, while the St. Ives Scrub rated much worse with ingredients like methylparaben and fragrance. Ironically, the CVS cleansing pads tested as a safer choice. Healthy products don't always cost more. Be your own label-reading detective!

Skip It!

SYNTHETIC FRAGRANCE OR CHEMICAL-LADEN FACIAL CLEANSER

THE UGLY

Parabens are common preservatives tied to skin irritation and immune system problems, and are found in some soap cleansers and other personal care products.

THE INCONVENIENT TRUTH

In 2004 the Environmental Working Group (EWG) found that 89% of 10,500 ingredients used in personal care products had not been evaluated for safety by any governing body.

BODY CARE

Green It!

PANGEA ORGANICS® BAR SOAPS / AUBREY ORGANICS® ROSA MOSQUETA CLEANSING BAR / DESERT ESSENCE® JOJOBA OIL

THE GOOD

The Desert Essence Pure Jojoba Oil is a pure and natural plant extract that can be used on your hair, skin, and scalp. It can remove makeup, cleanse clogged pores, prevent dandruff, and even be used as an aftershave moisturizer.

THE GREEN

Pangea Organics is a strong supporter of sustainable agriculture and culture and uses renewable, recycled, and recyclable resources in all of their fine products.

THE CONVENIENT TRUTH

When choosing personal care products, look for organic and fair trade options that don't have petroleum-based ingredients, sulfates, synthetic preservatives, or artificial color and fragrances.

Sage Advice

The Aubrey Organics company was the first personal care products manufacturer to list all ingredients in their products (1967) and also the first to be certified as an organic processor (1994). It has been delivering quality organic products for more than four decades.

Skip It!

NONORGANIC BODY WASH

THE UGLY

A 2008 study by the Organic Consumers Association (OCA) found the petrochemical carcinogenic contaminant 1,4-Dioxane in leading organic brand personal care products like body washes. Download a wallet guide from OCA and the Green Patriot Working Group to find safe products at: www.organicconsumers.org/bodycare/ShoppersSafetyGuide.pdf.

THE INCONVENIENT TRUTH

Known to cause cancer 1,4-dioxane is suspected as a kidney neurotoxicant, and respiratory toxicant.

Healthy Rx

To help avoid 1,4-dioxane in your personal care products, the Organic Consumers Association suggests consumers products with ingredient lists that have indications of ethoxylation. To find it look for: "myreth," "oleth," "laureth," "ceteareth," any other "eth," "PEG," "polyethylene," "polyethylene glycol," "polyoxyethylene," or "oxynol," in ingredient names on the product label. Known to cause cancer 1,4-dioxane is suspected as a kidney neurotoxicant, and respiratory toxicant.

PAIN REMEDIES

Green It!

SUMBODY®
HEADACHE, PMS, SINUS, AND INSOMNIA ZAPPER

THE GOOD

Zap away your daily doldrums. The Sumbody products are an all-natural solution to the aches and pains we all occasionally experience. They avoid the use of parabens, animal oils, sodium laurel/laureth sulfates, artificial preservatives, and synthetic chemicals.

THE GREEN

Take a pass on the side effects of pills and zap away those headaches, sinuses, PMS, insomnia, and other ailments the natural way. Apply to temples, neck, or chest, and gently inhale. Pure, refreshing essential oils and herbs will take the pain away and leave you feeling (and smelling) great!

THE CONVENIENT TRUTH

Choose products without side effects. In July 2009, the Food and Drug Administration advisory panel warned of liver damage from overuse of acetaminophen which is found in Nyquil, Theraflu, Tylenol, and Excedrin. It is the leading cause of acute liver failure in the U.S. with 1,600 cases a year.

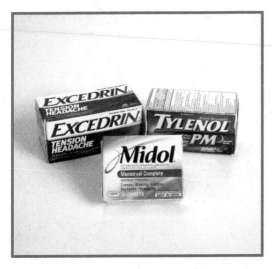

Healthy Rx

A minimum of one (too many) pharmaceutical drugs showed up in tests by the AP of 24 major metropolitan cities! Check the map to find out how your city water ranks at: hosted.ap.org/ specials/interactives/_national/pharmawater_update/index.html.

Skip It!
SYNTHETIC PAIN RELIEVERS

THE UGLY
The U.S. government does *not* regulate prescription drugs in tap water. But 250 million pounds of unused drugs and packaging are being disposed of annually by hospitals and long-term care facilities alone!

THE INCONVENIENT TRUTH
Estrogen, antibiotics, ibuprofen, and anti-anxiety medications in your tap water more than you bargained for? It is for the 41 million Americans who have a plethora of pharmaceuticals—including antibiotics, anti-convulsants, mood stabilizers, and sex hormones in their drinking water supplies, according to a 2008 investigation by the Associated Press.

INSECT REPELLENT

Green It!

BURT'S BEES® HERBAL INSECT REPELLENT / BUZZ AWAY® INSECT REPELLENT SPRAY OR TOWELLETTES

THE GOOD

It's easy to find safe, nontoxic bug repellant alternatives for you and your family.

THE GREEN

By using nontoxic insecticides, you not only protect yourself, you also eliminate the potential of toxic repellant getting washed down your drain and into the water supply.

THE CONVENIENT TRUTH

If you suspect you are going to be around mosquitoes, wear long pants and long sleeve shirts and make sure to tuck in your shirt and pants legs.

Sage Advice

Mosquitoes are often attracted to areas with standing water.

Skip It!

CHEMICAL-LADEN BUG REPELLENT

THE UGLY

Recent research shows that some insecticides are extremely dangerous and can cause severe and long-term illness.

THE INCONVENIENT TRUTH

The neurological toxin DEET is an active ingredient in many insect repellent products. In a study done on DEET, lab rats had no reaction to the toxin during the first 30 days, but after 60 days, the rats' brain cells started to die.

Sage Advice

DEET is used by one -third of the U.S. population every year; there is concern by scientists that DEET may collect in the sediment of streams and prove to be toxic to birds, fish, and other wildlife.

We do not inherit the earth
from our ancestors,
we borrow it from our children.

~ ANCIENT INDIAN PROVERB

CHAPTER 6

PLANES, TRAINS, AND AUTOMOBILES:

VACATION MEMORIES THROUGH A GREENER LENS

TRAVEL

Green It!

TERRAPASS AND NATIVE ENERGY

THE GOOD

Carbon Offsets are a great way for you to reduce your environmental impact. Many carbon footprint calculators are available online to help you recognize and lower your carbon footprint. You could make a huge impact in the fight against global warming just by modifying your personal behavior while utilizing offsets for the rest.

THE GREEN

Voluntary Carbon Standard (VCS) is a global benchmark standard for voluntary, project-based, greenhouse gas emission reductions and removals.

THE CONVENIENT TRUTH

By working with reputable carbon offset companies such as Native Energy (www. nativeenergy.com), Carbon Fund (www.carbonfund.org) or Terra Pass (www. terrapass.com), you can find ways to reduce your carbon footprint by purchasing carbon offsets, which in turn, fund clean energy and carbon reduction projects that help to reduce global warming. Clean Air-Cool Planet offers a consumer guide to these providers at: www. cleanair-coolplanet.org/ Consumers GuidetoCarbonOffsets.pdf.

Skip It!
TRADITIONAL TRAVEL

THE UGLY
Your "carbon footprint" represents the sum total of all the greenhouse gases you personally are responsible for putting into the Earth's atmosphere. For example, when you use energy from fossil fuels (oil or coal), you generate carbon dioxide (CO_2) emissions.

Mother Knows Best!

One way to reduce global warming is to reduce your carbon footprint through conservation. Common activity sources of carbon emissions are driving, flying, and home heating and cooling. Even the products you consume can contribute to your footprint because of the energy that was required to create and transport them across different states or countries.

Turn down or use a programmable thermostat, buy local produce, drive an energy efficient car or carpool, take the bike or public transportation and use energy saving products as solutions to reduce your personal carbon footprint.

THE INCONVENIENT TRUTH
The increase in global warming is attributed to the greenhouse gases we are putting into the atmosphere.

HOTELS
Green It!
GREENHOTELS.COM

THE GOOD
The majority of green hotels take conservational steps such as water/energy preservation and recycling to help reduce the use of natural resources.

THE GREEN
Environmentally friendly hotels not only save funds for the owner, but also allow the visitors to do their part for the environment.

THE CONVENIENT TRUTH
Locate a green hotel by visiting environmentallyfriendlyhotels.com or The Green Hotels Association at www.greenhotels.com.

Sage Advice
What "greens" a hotel? Energy-saving upgrades including LED bulbs water-saving appliances, and sheet changing cards. In addition, sustainable furniture and improvements related to better indoor air quality such as switching to green cleaners or using low-or no-VOC paints help the green report card.

Skip It!
TRADITIONAL / NON-GREEN ACCOMODATIONS

THE UGLY
When booking through popular travel websites and travel agencies, you are more apt to book a non-green hotel. Why is this concern? According to the American Hotel and Lodging Association Educational Institute, the hospitality industry spends $3.7 billion per year on energy consumption.

THE INCONVENIENT TRUTH
Not every hotel is practicing sustainable green practices, so you have to do a little bit of research to find those that are. You can also find hotels that are LEED (Leadership in Energy and Environmental Design) accredited by the U.S. Green Building Council at www.usgbc.org.

Mother Knows Best!
Dig deeper. For example, if you book a hotel stay through www.Orbitz.com, be sure that you are utilizing their eco-tourism section. Your purchase of eco-friendly accommodations, such as those with EPA's ENERGY STAR, use nearly 40% less energy than average buildings and emit 35% less carbon dioxide into the atmosphere. These actions will help make green hotels a standard option on travel websites and at agencies.

TRAVEL FOOD
Green It!
LAPTOP LUNCHES

THE GOOD
It's easy to eat healthy when you have your own food. Bringing organic apple slices or carrot sticks, nuts, or a healthy low fat protein bar are just some examples of great, portable snacks.

THE GREEN
Sorry Kermit, it is easy to be green. Bring your own reusable bottle with a beverage you know is healthy. This will eliminate another disposable cup from going into our landfill. Also try laptop lunches which fit perfectly on the airplane tray table. They are Bento-Style reusable boxes that are recyclable, dishwasher safe and contain no phthalates, Bisphenol A (BPA), or lead. Visit: www.laptoplunches.com.

THE CONVENIENT TRUTH
Don't accept snacks like peanuts and pretzels that you are not going to eat and just throw away on the plane or at the airport. It has been estimated that nationwide, U.S. airports generated 425,000 tons of waste in 2004 and this is expected to increase up 45% by 2015 according to NRDC.

Skip It!
NONORGANIC FOOD IN DISPOSABLE PACKAGING

THE UGLY
The U.S. airline industry discards enough aluminum cans each year to build 58 Boeing 747 airplanes, according to NRDC's research project Trash Landings, and reportedly discarded 9,000 tons of plastic in 2004.

THE INCONVENIENT TRUTH
Don't drink the coffee! In 2008 the EPA stated that "airline passengers with compromised immune systems or others concerned may want to request canned or bottled beverages, and avoid drinking coffee, tea, and other drinks prepared with tap water."

Mother Knows Best!
Pass on the ice cubes next time you are on an airline. In 2004, the EPA found that 15% of the 327 aircrafts' water systems they tested were positive for coliform. As a response to this finding, the EPA started a process to adjust the existing regulations for aircraft public water systems. In 2008, EPA proposed the Aircraft Drinking Water Rule for public review and comment. To be on the safe side, it's probably best to avoid adding ice from the plane to your beverage.

CELL PHONES
Green It!
AIR TUBE HEADSET

THE GOOD
Cell-cycle your phone! You can donate or recycle old cell phones through these web sites: www.cellphonesfor soldiers.com, www.wirelessrecycling. com, www.collectivegood.com, www. eco-cell.com, or earn some green at www.Cellfor Cash.com.

THE GREEN
Over 100 million cell phones are unused in the U.S. By recycling your mobile phone you are helping to reduce greenhouse gas emissions. Before recycling, be sure to remove your personal information first! Recent studies point out that 99% of recycled cell phones contain personal information. Enlist the help of U.S. based ReCellular (www.recellular. com) to help guarantee removal.

THE CONVENIENT TRUTH
Get a solar cell phone charger and avoid the hassle of having to plug it in, at www.solio.com.

Sage Advice
Independent studies have revealed that Air Tube Technology delivers sound from your cell phone through an air-filled wireless tube that can reduce the amount of electromagnetic radiation reaching your head.

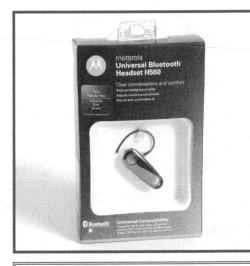

Skip It!
DIRECT EAR ANTENNA / NON-AIR TUBE HEADSET

THE UGLY

It has been estimated that we are 100 million times more exposed to electromagnetic radiation and microwaves than our grandparents.

A 2006 study of regular cell phone users determined a 60% increased risk of glioma (a cancer that starts in the brain or spine).

THE INCONVENIENT TRUTH

Clinical and laboratory studies have revealed that the EMFs (electromagnetic fields) emitted from your cell phone are linked to hazardous health conditions including: headaches, sleep disturbance, brain tumors, Alzheimer's, Parkinson's, altered memory function, concentration, and spatial awareness as well as other types of cancer.

Healthy Rx

Radio frequency (RF) from wireless devices has been shown to interfere with the body's immune system. Younger people are more vulnerable to direct cell phone to ear contact because their skulls are still developing. Limit the use of your cell phone and use the built in speakerphone feature or an air tube headset with your cell phone to reduce your potential exposure. A 2009 study of over 1,000 cell phones rates phones by radiation levels. Find yours at: ewg.org/cellphone-radiation.

CAR RENTAL

Green It!

RENT A HYBRID

THE GOOD

It is getting easier to find and rent flex fuel or hybrid vehicles. Car rental companies like Enterprise, National, and Alamo are leading the trend in offering planet-friendly car options at many of their locations.

THE GREEN

Try to rent the smallest car that fits your needs for the trip. On average this will help you save on fuel costs and cut down on CO_2 emissions compared to using a larger vehicle.

THE CONVENIENT TRUTH

Driving the speed limit will save you gas money. Driving at 75 mph instead of 65 mph will cause you to lower your fuel economy by almost 10%.

Sage Advice

Only patronize gas stations that have vapor-recovery nozzles (distinguishable by the accordion-looking black plastic that is attached to the nozzle). They help recover the vapors of the fuels from getting into the air and ultimately our atmosphere.

Skip It!
SUVs / GAS GUZZLING VECHICLES

THE UGLY
Automobile exhaust from motor vehicles still accounts for a significant portion of air pollution. SUVs are no match to hybrid cars, according to Clean Air-Cool Planet, since hybrids use approximately 80% less pollutants than non-hybrid vehicles.

THE INCONVENIENT TRUTH
In the year 2030 it is predicted that the current global oil production of 81 million barrels a day is going to fall too just 39 million barrels because of diminishing resources.

Mother Knows Best!
Fuel spills at gas stations can lead to gasoline polluting our water supply and ultimately hurting wildlife. Avoid unnecessary spills by not overfilling your tank. This often happens when someone attempts to top off with extra gasoline after the automated nozzle clicks off.

VACATIONS
Green It!
HOME EXCHANGE

THE GOOD

You can save the money from staying in hotels by using www.Home Exchange.com or Home Base Holidays (www.homebase-hols.com) on your next vacation. Membership allows members to coordinate alternate visits to each other's homes.

THE GREEN

About half of the members even share cars, reducing the need to rent a vehicle.

THE CONVENIENT TRUTH

By staying in the comfort of a home in a local community, you have more opportunities to experience local life than you would by staying in a motel or hotel.

Sage Advice

Many of the members exchange their second homes. In fact the website even allows for a search function that only lists second homes for exchange.

Skip It!

HIGH-PRICED HOTEL

THE UGLY

In the 2008 annual Vacation Costs Survey by AAA (American Auto-mobile Association), they recommended travel budgets of $244 per day for lodging and meals for two adults traveling in North America.

THE INCONVENIENT TRUTH

Many larger hotels dispose of up to 8 tons of waste per day.

Sage Advice

Don't like the idea of staying at a stranger's home? Take a "staycation"—a period of time off when you relax and enjoy local area attractions from your own home. Staycations have become very popular with the rise of gas prices and other expenses of vacation travel. Staycation's popularity allowed for its addition to the 2009 version of the Merriam-Webster's Collegiate Dictionary.

CAR FRESHENER

Green It!

LAVENDER SACHETS UNDER THE SEAT

THE GOOD

Purchase or make your own eco-friendly lavender sachets (cotton sachet filled with sweet-smelling organic lavender) which can be placed under the seat of your car, rather than using chemical filled air fresheners that most car washes offer.

THE GREEN

You will avoid potential exposure to phthalates (known hormone disrupters) when you use natural essential oils or other eco-friendly options versus toxic car air fresheners.

THE CONVENIENT TRUTH

Instead of a sachet you can create a spray. Just fill a mister bottle with water, and then add a few drops of your favorite organic essential oil, such as sandalwood or ylang ylang, to help improve the scent of your car.

Sage Advice

Another eco-friendlier car freshener option is the AromaCar Commuter Kit by Vim Essentials. The kit comes with everything you need. Just place a few drops of essential oil on its biodegradable felt pad, put it in the reusable diffuser, and plug it in your car. In just moments you will experience the healthy aroma of scents like mint, bergamot, ginger, or other favorites.

Skip It!
SYNTHETIC / SCENED AIR FRESHENER

THE UGLY
Many synthetic car fresheners contain phthalates. Studies have suggested that prolonged exposure to certain kinds of phthalates can cause cancer and developmental and even sex-hormone abnormalities.

THE INCONVENIENT TRUTH
Don't try to cover up cigarette smoke in your car. A German study revealed that smoking in the car with car air fresheners increases the risk of cancer due to a dangerous chemical interaction between the smoke and the air freshener scents.

Mother Knows Best!
A hot car can make your car smell even worse. To combat this use a windshield shade to help avoid the build up of summer heat. It will also help you keep frost off your window during cold winter months.

CAR WASH
Green It!

LUCKY EARTH
WATERLESS CARWASH

THE GOOD
Commercial carwash facilities are required to drain their wastewater into sewer systems for treatment prior to discharge back into the great outdoors, according to U.S. and Canadian law.

- -

THE GREEN
While many commercial car washes also recycle and re-use the rinse water, they also use computer-controlled systems and high-pressure nozzles and pumps that minimize water usage.

- -

THE CONVENIENT TRUTH
An industry group representing commercial car wash companies, The International Carwash Association, reports that automatic car washes use less than 50% of the amount of water even the most careful home car washers use.

- -

Lisa's D.I.Y.
Don't have time to take your wheels to the wash? No problem. You can use a waterless car wash system without harming the environment and have a clean car in approximately half an hour. Look for the Lucky Earth starter kit that contains a 32oz waterless car wash, 16 oz tire shine, and 4 microfiber towels.

Skip It!

WASHING CAR AT HOME

THE UGLY
While a commercial car wash averages less than 45 gallons per car, washing a car at home typically uses between 80 and 140 gallons of water.

THE INCONVENIENT TRUTH
Most car wash and car polish ingredients contain petroleum distillates. These are associated with irritation to the skin, eyes, nose, and lungs. Check the labels and avoid those marked "Danger," "Harmful," or "Fatal."

Healthy Rx

Waterless systems like Freedom and Lucky Earth Waterless Car Wash are environmentally friendly solutions to getting your car clean. Lucky Earth is a solution that cleans all solid surfaces such as paint, glass, fiberglass, plastic, and chrome, and can be used on wet or dry surfaces. The Lucky Earth process consists of organic soaps/surfactants and other high-quality organic ingredients that dissolve dirt and create a nonstick surface while being environmentally safe, hypo-allergenic, VOC free, dye free, fragrance free, and paraben free.

HAND SANITIZER

Green It!

HAND SANZ™ BY ALL TERRAIN® / FOR MY KIDS™ HAND WASH / THIEVES® SANITIZER, WIPES & SOAP

THE GOOD

Almost good enough to eat! Thieves brand hand sanitizer consists of peppermint essential oil, which is used to denature the ethanol in this product versus the synthetic chemicals commonly found in hand sanitizers. Other ingredients include clove, eucalyptus radiata, cinnamon, rosemary, and lemon.

THE GREEN

All Terrain Hand Sanz is all natural and biodegradable. This natural sanitizer kills 99.9% of germs and bacteria without chemicals.

THE CONVENIENT TRUTH

An alternative is EO Hand Sanitizer which is a biodegradable, organic, plant-based sanitizer consisting of certified organic alcohol and certified organic lavender essential oil.

Sage Advice

Approximately $1 billion is spent per year on antimicrobial products.

Skip It!

SYNTHETIC CHEMICAL / ARTIFICIALLY SCENTED ANTIBACTERIAL SANITIZERS

THE UGLY

Most traditional hand sanitizers contain over 60% of ethyl alcohol or isopropanol, synthetic fragrance, Propylene glycol and parabens.

THE INCONVENIENT TRUTH

Antibacterial overload! Avoid products containing triclosan, a disinfectant found in many antibacterial products. It is also found under the trade names Microban and Biofresh.

Studies have increasingly linked triclosan to a range of health and environmental effects, from skin irritation and allergy susceptibility to bacterial and compounded antibiotic resistance.

Healthy Rx

Err on the side of caution and avoid overuse of antibacterial products. Try hot water, plain soap, and a bit of elbow grease or healthier options of hand sanitizers.

SUNSCREEN

Green It!

BADGER® / CALIFORNIA BABY® / JANE IREDALE®

THE GOOD
White zinc oxide does not irritate skin and has not been linked with any environmental or health problems. For a benzophenone-free product, try California Baby SPF 30+ Sunscreen.

THE GREEN
SPF stands for Sun Protection Factor. This measures how effectively a sunscreen protects the skin against UVB rays, but does not include information about harmful UVA (long wave) linked to photo aging and skin cancers like melanoma. Look for a broad or multi spectrum protection for both UVA and UVB rays.

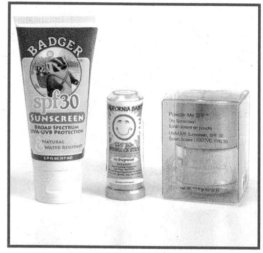

THE CONVENIENT TRUTH
UVB (short wave rays) are the type of radiation that causes sunburn. UV radiation contributes to some types of skin cancer including basal and squamous cell carcinomas.

Skip It!

ARTIFICALLY FRAGRANCED OR CHEMICAL-LADEN SUNSCREEN AND SUNBLOCK

THE UGLY
Chemicals from sunscreen absorb into your blood stream, placing excess strain on your liver. Conventional sunscreens and even some natural sunscreens contain harmful chemicals including: artificial fragrance, artificial colors and synthetic preservatives.

THE INCONVENIENT TRUTH
More than a million cases of skin cancer are diagnosed in the U.S. every year. The incidence of malignant melanoma, the most dangerous form of the disease, is escalating.

Healthy Rx
Avoid suspected carcinogens in ingredients including: diethanolamin, (DEA, TEA), padimate-o, and titanium dioxide. Other ingredients to avoid are suspected endocrine (hormone) disrupters: benzophenone (oxybenzone), homosalate, octyl-methoxycinnamate (octinoxate), and parabens (methyl-, ethyl-, butyl-, propyl-). Finally, to enjoy sunnier days and prevent skin irritation and rashes, avoid sunscreens that contain chemicals such as avobenzone, benzophenone, octyl-methoxycinnamate, and PABA (para-aminobenzoic acid).

As the bee collects nectar and
departs without injuring
the flower, or its color or
scent, so let a sage dwell
in the community.

-BUDDHA

CHAPTER 7

THE 9 TO 5 GREENED

STEPS TO REDUCE COSTS AT WORK, BREATHE CLEANER AIR, AND ENJOY HAPPIER HOURS

PACKING MATERIALS

Green It!

BIODEGRADEABLE PACKING PEANUTS

THE GOOD
If you don't have environmentally friendly packing material on hand, opt for old newspaper since it is both recyclable and biodegradable.

THE GREEN
Environmentally friendly, starch-based peanuts are biodegradable and dissolve in water. They can be washed down the drain or placed in a compost pile.

THE CONVENIENT TRUTH
PaperNuts (www.papernuts.com) are another example of a loose fill that is made from 100% recycled materials, and is both biodegradable and fully recyclable.

Sage Advice
The best way to handle Styrofoam peanuts is to make sure they get reused. Call the Peanut Hotline at 800-828-2214 to find out a drop off location near you, or take them to a local shipping business like UPS or Mailbox Etc. for reuse.

Skip It!

STYROFOAM PACKING PEANUTS

THE UGLY
Styrofoam, also known as expanded polystyrene (EPS) foam, does not biodegrade.

THE INCONVENIENT TRUTH
EPS may not be heavy since 98% is actually air, but the volume of the material takes up quite a bit of space in our landfills.

Sage Advice
Unfortunately, EPS is huge problem with our marine life. The expanded polystyrene foam, like most plastic, floats in water and when disposed of as litter, it ultimately gets into our marine eco-system. In fact, plastic, including EPS, comprises 90% of floating marine debris according to the Clean Water Action of California. EPS will often photodegrade and breakdown into smaller pieces that marine animals mistaken for food, contributing to an even bigger problem than merely filling up our landfills.

INK CARTRIDGES

Green It!

REFILLABLE INK CARTRIDGES

THE GOOD
Spend up to 75% less on ink cartridges, by refilling cartridges to save money and resources.

THE GREEN
Make some green from your old cartridges. CastleInk.com has a recycle program with Capital Imaging that pays you $4.00 for every "virgin" (i.e., non-refilled) cartridge you return.

Look for remanufactured cartridges that use recycled cartridges and refilled ink reservoirs. Or, save more ink by printing drafts of less important documents. Try setting your printer to "draft mode."

THE CONVENIENT TRUTH
Easy tip to save your print head: When your computer alerts you that the cartridge is low on ink, refill it immediately. Continuing to print may damage your print head.

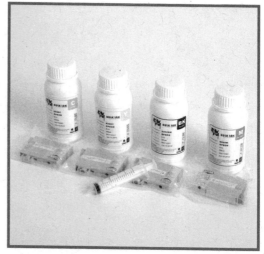

Lisa's D.I.Y.
At Walgreens you can refill your ink cartridges and save your money. Take it to the photo counter and they'll refill while you wait. They service: Dell, HP, Lexmark, Okidata, Primera, Sharp, and Xerox cartridges.

Skip It!
NON-REFILLABLE INK CARTRIDGE

THE UGLY
In the U.S., over 350 million empty ink and toner cartridges are thrown out every year, according to www.ink guides.com.

THE INCONVENIENT TRUTH
Besides being costly, ink cartridges are not earth friendly. They take 450 years to decompose in our landfills.

Sage Advice
Sometimes your printer may not recognize that the ink cartridge is filled. You may need to reset the printer and/or select the option that says new cartridge.

When you are done with a cartridge, be sure to take advantage of take back programs offered by manufacturers for recycling. For example, Staples offers a program for HP, Lexmark or Dell cartridges. When returned to their store for recycling, a $3.00 Staple Rewards is given toward a future purchase of ink or toner. They also offer a service called Ink Drop. When your cartridge is finished, mail it back to Staples in the prepaid envelope. They'll send a replacement free of shipping costs.

BUILDINGS

Green It!

WALKING UP STAIRS

THE GOOD
Take the stairs! A 154-pound person burns 10 calories per minute when ascending, and 7 calories per minute when descending a flight of stairs.

THE GREEN
Another way to make a difference in conserving energy in your building is to make sure everything in the office is powered down during off hours. For example, individual office lights, computers, printers, and other office equipment can put a drain on the electricity use of the building when left on unnecessarily.

THE CONVENIENT TRUTH
It has been estimated that for every $1 invested in energy efficiency of a building, the asset value increases by an estimated $3.

Sage Advice
KONE elevators, one of the world's leading elevator companies, is targeting a 50% energy consumption cutback in its elevator offering by the year 2010, compared to its previous elevator offering.

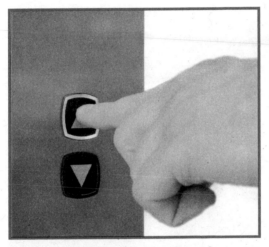

Skip It!
WASTEFUL ENERGY CONSUMPTION

THE UGLY
U.S. office buildings account for 28% of commercial energy demand, according to the Department of Energy.

THE INCONVENIENT TRUTH
Elevators in North American office buildings usually use between 3 to 5% of the building's electricity.

Sage Advice
In the state of California, the buildings sector uses approximately 66% of the electric energy. California's Flex Your Power indicates that electricity consumption in buildings doubled between 1989 and 2005 and at the current rate, by the year 2030 the electricity demand in buildings will increase 150%. This consumption equates to a staggering 23 million megawatt-hours (MWh) of electricity each year.

California businesses collectively spend more than $15 billion a year on heating, cooling, lighting and other energy uses.

COMMUTING
Green It!
CARPOOL

THE GOOD
The U.S. Department of Transportation and the EPA are teaming up with businesses to set up Commuter Choice programs. The programs are designed to help cut pollution, reduce traffic congestion, and conserve energy.

THE GREEN
In addition to carpooling, public transit can be another great solution. By taking the bus or train you are sharing resources with your local community, and ultimately helping to reduce pollution.

THE CONVENIENT TRUTH
If your employer doesn't have a Commuter Choice program, ask them to start one. Go to commuterchoice.com

----

CARPOOLS ONLY
2 OR MORE PERSONS
PER VEHICLE

Ron's Green $$ Tip
By utilizing greener commuting through the Commuter Choice programs, you won't just be helping the environment; you may be eligible for cash and other benefits. Some of the programs offer workers tax-free transit or vanpool benefits that are up to $100 per month.

Sage Advice

You should never chose premium, high-octane fuels if your car doesn't require it. You would just be wasting your money, because it does nothing to improve the performance or fuel economy of your vehicle according to the American Council for an Energy-Efficient Economy (ACEEE).

Skip It!
SOCIALLY IRRESPONSIBLE COMMUTING

THE UGLY

Transportation is responsible for about 70% of all the petroleum used in the U.S. In addition, most the energy we use for transportation is used to power light-duty cars and trucks for personal transportation (around 59%). This appears to be a growing problem because since 2003 the U.S. has had registered more private cars than licensed drivers.

THE INCONVENIENT TRUTH

According to the U.S. Chamber of Commerce Institute for 21st Century Energy, the United States is currently 96% reliant on petroleum for its transportation.

BUSINESS

Green It!

VIDEO CONFERENCING

THE GOOD

Why travel for business when you can use Skype for free? Save time, energy, and money. With Skype you can conference and video call free from your computer. The only set-up needed is a webcam, headset, and broadband connection. For more information on Skype services go to www.skype.com.

THE GREEN

With free video calls you can talk face-to-face with clients, reduce air travel, and reduce unnecessary carbon emissions into the environment.

THE CONVENIENT TRUTH

In addition to reducing business travel, video conferencing from a home office can make effective tele-commuting a reality as well. Meetings done via video conferencing will reduce the gas consumption of employees required to travel to a central office location while allowing more effective use of employee's time.

Sage Advice

With Skype you can also keep costs down when calling numbers abroad. However, you shouldn't replace your entire phone service with Skype, because it does not offer the ability to call emergency services if you are need of help.

CONFERENCES/ TRAVEL

Sage Advice

The average business meeting produces 20 pounds of waste per person (common examples include plastic, aluminum, and glass containers and paper and food waste) and many larger meetings take place at hotel conference rooms utilizing additional energy.

Skip It!
UNNECESSARY BUSINESS TRAVEL

THE UGLY

An estimated 405 million long-distance business trips are being flown by Americans every year according to the U.S. Bureau of Travel Statistics. If you must travel, use carbon offsets for your travel. They are available through Expedia, Travelocity, and most airlines, including Jet Blue, United, and Delta. Or, use offset companies like Native Energy, Terra Pass, or Carbonfund. These can help alleviate the 7% of CO_2 emissions generated from the worldwide air travel each year.

THE INCONVENIENT TRUTH

Often referred to as Radiative Forcing, greenhouse gas emissions produced higher in the atmosphere (e.g., air travel) are worse than emissions at ground level according to some scientists.

PAPER

Green It!

POST-CONSUMER RECYCLED CONTENT OR TOTALLY CHLORINE-FREE PAPER

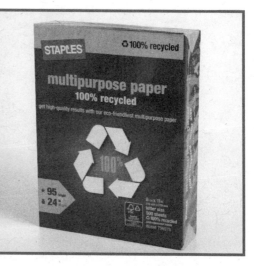

THE GOOD
Drive a thousand miles on a cleaner conscience: 39 gallons of gasoline is saved with every ton of paper recycled.

THE GREEN
For a smaller environmental footprint, use chlorine free paper.

THE CONVENIENT TRUTH
Post-consumer recycled, chlorine-free paper is readily available at most office supplies stores.

Lisa's D.I.Y.
Cut down on paper being used in the office by 50% just by printing double-sided sheets. With the average office employee averaging 10,000 sheets of paper per year, that would save 5,000 sheets of paper. If you want to go further, reduce the margins of what is printed from 1" to 0.5".

For more green office tips check out The9to5Greened.com.

Skip It!

NON-POST-CONSUMER-RECYCLED CONTENT OR PAPER PRODUCED WITH CHLORINE

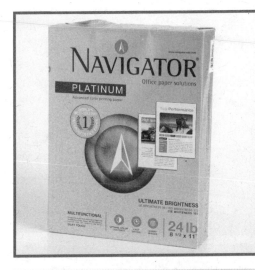

THE UGLY

At least 40% of trash, making up the largest component of municipal solid waste going into our landfills, consists of paper. This contributes more than any other type of waste.

THE INCONVENIENT TRUTH

Water pollution, deforestation, and demolished animal habitats are all consequences in the production of paper.

Mother Knows Best!

If you must use virgin paper, use it in moderation and be sure to recycle it, as it does the most damage to the environment.

ELECTRICAL DEVICES

Green It!

SURGE PROTECTOR

THE GOOD

It's easy to save energy by going green! Many states already offer you the opportunity to utilize green power. To find out where you can buy green power in your state, go to the U.S. Department of Energy Green Power Network at www.eere. energy. gov/greenpower/buying/buying_pow er.shtml.

THE GREEN

You can save time, money, and energy when you use the Smart Strip brand power strip for your computer, fax, printers, and other computer equipment. It offers superior surge protection and is a prefect solution to bulky transformer plug-ins. The power strips have built-in programs that allow them to "sense" when a device is off or on by the flow of electrical current through the strips control outlet. It then turns off selected equipment when it's not in use—so you won't waste electricity.

THE CONVENIENT TRUTH

Notebook computers use less energy than desktops, and when you put them on system standby, it reduces their power from 20 to 30 watts all the way down to 1 to 2 watts. Significant indeed!

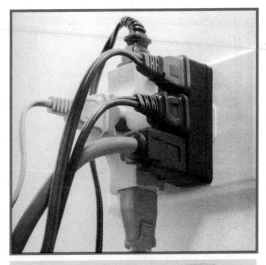

Mother Knows Best!

Use "green power," a power that is generated from renewable energy sources like solar and wind. When you chose green power, you are choosing an environmentally preferred source for your home's electricity. If you don't have the ability to make the change at your local utility, don't worry, you can still purchase RECs (renewable energy certificates). These certificates represent environmental attributes of power produced from renewable energy projects, and they allow you the flexibility not to have to switch electricity suppliers.

Skip It!
NOT USING A SURGE PROTECTOR

THE UGLY
Some electrical devices (ex: computers, power adapters, coffeemakers to name a few) can still be using electricity even when they are turned off. This is referred to as a "standby power," "idle current," or "phantom load."

THE INCONVENIENT TRUTH
On average, 40% of the energy used in offices today is from electronics that are powered off but are still plugged in.

MONITORS

Green It!

ENERGY STAR LCD MONITORS

THE GOOD

Sleep *is* recommended at the office—at least for your monitor! Set your computer to switch to sleep mode after 5 minutes of idle time.

THE GREEN

Look for electronic items that have Energy Star certification, alternatively powered electronics, and those containing recycled material.

THE CONVENIENT TRUTH

By enabling sleep mode, you can reduce energy consumption—especially in older models!

With the display in a low power state vs. an active state, a monitor will typically consume 1 to 3 watts of power. LCD monitors consume much less power than a CRT display, at 15 to 60 watts versus 50 to 125 watts of power. Sometimes less really is more!

Lisa's D.I.Y.

Got at least 5 electronic items or more to dispose of? Californian's can use www.recycle4free.net to recycle old electronics. The company will pick them up from your location, remove your data, and properly recycle at no cost to you.

Skip It!
CRT COMPUTER MONITORS

THE UGLY
Approximately 5 to 8 pounds of lead is found in conventional CRT monitors.

THE INCONVENIENT TRUTH
Replace old electronics. If all old electronics were replaced with new electric-saving technology, it would be equivalent to taking 2.7 million cars off the road during the computer's lifetime.

Mother Knows Best!

Greenpeace (www.greenpeace.org) has created "The Guide to Greener Electronics," which ranks companies (0–10; zero being the worst) on a tightened set of chemicals and e-waste criteria, and on new energy criteria. HP, Lenovo, and Dell failed to deliver their promise of eliminating vinyl plastic (PVC) and brominated flame retardants (BFRs) from their products by the end of 2009. Nokia keeps the top spot with new CO_2 emissions reduction targets.

Until man duplicates
a blade of grass, nature can
laugh at his so called
scientific knowledge.

-Thomas Edison

CHAPTER 8

GUILTLESS HOLIDAYS

UNIVERSAL TIPS FOR GREENING YOUR HOLIDAY HOME

CHRISTMAS TREES

Green It!

LIVE
CHRISTMAS TREES

THE GOOD
Real trees absorb carbon dioxide, emit oxygen, and can be replanted in your yard or recycled after the holidays.

THE GREEN
Don't live in the mountains? No worries. Get one delivered to your door from LivingChristmasTrees.org.

THE CONVENIENT TRUTH
The plastic material in artificial Christmas trees is typically made from PVC, which can be a potential source of hazardous lead. The good news is that lead test kits are readily available at most hardware stores, and they are very easy to use. In under a minute you can determine if your fake tree is lead free.

Lisa's D.I.Y.
It's free to have your real tree recycled. Contact your local city government for specific tree-collection days or enter your zip code in at Earth911.org. Do not use your regular curbside pickup. The tree will just end up in a landfill where it can take up to three decades to decompose!

Healthy Rx

The potential for lead poising from Christmas trees is so significant that California Proposition 65 requires artificial trees manufactured in China to have a warning label indicating the lead content.

Skip It!
ARTIFICIAL / PLASTIC CHRISTMAS TREES

THE UGLY

Most artificial trees are made of the #3 plastic, polyvinyl chloride, which fuses vinyl chloride molecules with toxic metals such as lead and cadmium. These toxic substances can leach from the plastic and be digested when a child or pet chews on them. As the plastic degrades under normal conditions, exposure to lead can occur, typically when the tree is nine years or older. Lead is a neurotoxin that can cause severe damage to the nervous system, especially in children.

THE INCONVENIENT TRUTH

Dubbed the most toxic plastic, PVC is a nonrenewable petroleum byproduct and cannot be recycled.

ORNAMENTS

Green It!
GLASS OR WOODEN CHRISTMAS ORNAMENTS

THE GOOD
Think outside the Christmas gift box: trim the tree with wooden or fabric ornaments and paper chains.

THE GREEN
Try an old-fashioned Christmas with gingerbread ornaments and popcorn strings. Avoid plastics that are made from nonrenewable petrochemicals and take years to biodegrade.

THE CONVENIENT TRUTH
Opt for wooden or glass ornaments instead of plastic, which can contain toxic chemicals, contribute to pollution in production, and end up as landfill waste.

Ron's Green $$ Tip
Make snowflake ornaments from the backside of your own recycled white paper or a recycled brand that is available at your local office supply store.

Skip It!
PLASTIC AND IMPORTED METAL ORNAMENTS

THE UGLY
Beware of metal ornaments from China that may contain lead, or polymer clay-derived ones. Polymer clays are usually made of PVC, a plastic that contains phthalates, which have been linked to cancer and reproductive effects.

THE INCONVENIENT TRUTH
Stuck in a tinsel time warp? Tinsel is made from aluminum fused to polyvinyl chloride (PVC) plastic, and therefore is not recyclable or bio-degradable. If you already own tinsel, check with your local hazardous waste collection to see if they will accept it. Learn more at www.epa. gov/waste/conserve/materials/hhw.htm.

Healthy Rx
Use less plastic and more green by decorating with Poinsettias, Norfolk Island pines, or a Christmas cactus. Why? According to a study by NASA scientists, these 3 plants not only add oxygen to your air but actually remove toxins and chemical vapors. Keep 'em year-round for cleaner indoor air.

HOLIDAY LIGHTS

Green It!

LED CHRISTMAS TREE LIGHTS

THE GOOD

Available in almost every color, shape, and size—and at practically every retailer—LEDs last for thousands of hours, according to Energy Star. The upfront cost is higher but will save you a bundle of green in utility costs.

THE GREEN

LED (light-emitting diode), the same technology that lights the display on your watch or calculator, converts energy into light rather than heat. They are 90% more efficient than incandescent bulbs. By converting 90% of their energy into light, only 10% of the LED energy is utilized as heat versus incandescent bulbs, which do the opposite; they convert only 10% of energy into light while the remaining 90% is wasted as heat. In

fact, LED bulbs last up to 10 times longer than compact fluorescents bulbs.

THE CONVENIENT TRUTH

Got a burnt out light bulb? No worries if you are using LED string lights. When one LED bulb burns out, it doesn't affect the rest of the string of lights.

Skip It!

INCANDESCENT CHRISTMAS TREE LIGHTS

THE UGLY

Incandescent bulbs generate heat, therefore can pose a fire risk. LEDs, on the other hand, emit very little heat, stay cool to the touch, and hence, are less of a fire hazard.

THE INCONVENIENT TRUTH

Incandescent lights waste energy and cost you more to use in the long run. It is estimated if everyone replaced the incandescent lights on their trees with LEDs, enough energy would be saved each Christmas to heat 200,000 homes for a year!

Mother Knows Best!

You can also add solar powered holiday lights to your outdoor decorations; they don't require electricity, but rely on a small solar grid. They are becoming more widely available and are offered in a variety of colors and styles.

HOLIDAY CARDS & PAPER

Green It!

BLOOMIN FLOWER® CARDS / PLEASAN-TREES® / RECYCLED WRAPPING PAPER

THE GOOD

Create a new tradition to skip the wrapping paper and bows altogether. Instead, send everyone on a treasure hunt to find their gifts!

- -

THE GREEN

Using old newspaper or maps for wrapping a package will never go out of style and is also very handy in a pinch. Prefer gift bags? Wrapsacks.com makes trackable, reusable cloth gift bags—you can follow online to see where they end up next!

- -

THE CONVENIENT TRUTH

Focus on giving back by donating used cards to a senior center, school,

or recreation center for use as craft supplies. Or add shredded cards to your compost bin as another way to recycle and reuse holiday waste.

- -

Lisa's D.I.Y.

Wrap gifts in the Sunday comics or kids' artwork.

Use cinnamon sticks and raffia for a decorative touch on gifts instead of ribbons and bows.

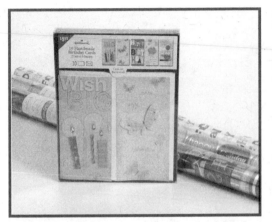

Mother Knows Best!

Use recycled paper, gifted gift bags, or give cards that can be planted like those from Bloomin' Flower Cards (with embedded seeds and printed with soy inks) or recycled cards from Pleasantrees.

Card fronts can be stored in a box for future Christmas art projects, such as placemats, wreaths, new cards, gift tags, or ornaments.

Send personalized photo cards the environmentally friendly way. With www.ReProduct.net's new Photo Card selection, simply upload your photos, choose your style, greeting, and background, and they'll do the rest!

Skip It!

NON-RECYCLED CARDS & WRAPPING PAPER / TOXIC INKS

THE UGLY

According to Hallmark, 2 billion cards are sent each year during the holidays, most of which will end up in landfills.

THE INCONVENIENT TRUTH

In the U.S. we generate an additional 5 million tons of waste during the holidays, accounting for 25% more waste than any other time of year. Four million tons of the waste is from wrapping paper and shopping bags.

OUTDOOR LIGHTING

Green It!
SOLAR
OUTDOOR LIGHTS

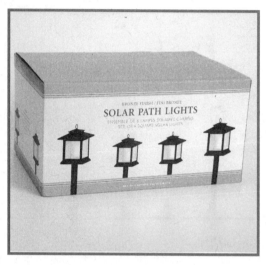

THE GOOD
It is easy to install outdoor solar lights, and they are virtually maintenance-free.

THE GREEN
Solar power lighting is a great renewable energy source, with little or no emission of pollutants.

THE CONVENIENT TRUTH
Home outdoor solar lighting products are readily available at most hardware, home improvement, or lighting stores.

Sage Advice
Outdoor solar lights convert and store electricity from just a few hours of sunlight during the day and then use the power for later that night. Also try installing motion detectors in less used areas or use timers to ensure lights are turned off when no one is at home.

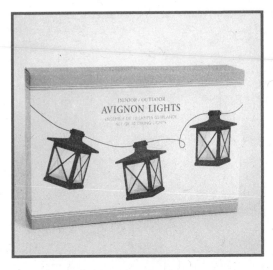

Sage Advice

This year the U.S. can reduce its global warming pollutant emissions to 10% below 1990 levels just by taking appropriate energy-saving measures, according to the Energy Innovations report.

Skip It!
AC-POWERED EXTERIOR LIGHTING

THE UGLY
According to Solar Energy International (SEI), America uses about 15 times more energy per person than does the typical developing country.

THE INCONVENIENT TRUTH
AC-powered exterior lighting can be inflexible due to the constraints of running low-voltage wires. Solar options are even easier to maintain and have fewer limitations for use in larger landscapes.

HANUKKAH

Green It!

LED MENORAH

THE GOOD

Hanukkah, also known as the Festival of Lights, is one of the most joyous and celebratory times of the Jewish religion's year.

THE GREEN

Choose wax candles for the Menorah that are made from vegetable-based wax, are biodegradable and contain no petroleum.

THE CONVENIENT TRUTH

Use less wax with a battery-powered Menorah. Just turn on the super bright LED bulb lights versus burning candles. Find one at: www.zion-judaica.com.

Lisa's D.I.Y.

Make your own eco-friendly Dreidel from recycled cardboard, paper, or cartons.

Skip It!
NON-LED
PLASTIC MENORAH

THE UGLY
Nothing is ugly about this celebration, but there are environmental concerns around the festivities. For example, the burning of petroleum-based paraffin candles in menorahs utilize limited resources while synthetic fragrances can be toxic to the air we breathe. Disposable dreidels that are not eco-friendly can create problem waste.

THE INCONVENIENT TRUTH
According to The Green Hanukkah Campaign, every menorah (natural or synthetic) candle produces approximately 15 grams of CO_2, which can be significant with all the candle lighting during the celebration.

Sage Advice
The Green Hanukkah Campaign is a controversial movement to stop the burning of candles during the celebration in order to prevent the release of large amounts of carbon dioxide that are ultimately harming our environment.

VALENTINE'S DAY

Green It!

ENDANGERED SPECIES® CHOCOLATE / GLOBAL EXCHANGE® CHOCOLATE / CHOCO-LATL® CHOCOLATE

THE GOOD
Need a saucy idea? Check out Raw Chocolate Sauce from Chocolatl, made with raw, organic, fair trade ingredients, and the packaging is 100% biodegradable.

THE GREEN
Eat endangered Species or Dabble with Dagoba organic chocolates. Dagoba promotes sustainable cocoa economies and utilizes cacao instead of sugar.

THE CONVENIENT TRUTH
Global Exchange efforts promotes Fair Trade certified chocolate, which pays fair wages, prohibits forced and abusive child labor, and ensures environmentally sustainable production methods are met.

Ron's Green $$ Tip
Looking for a less commercialized and more affordable way to express your love? The EPA suggests green tips like sending electronic cards and making new cards from scrap paper or by attaching new backs to the fronts of old cards.

Skip It!
NONORGANIC CHOCOLATE

THE UGLY
In West Africa's cocoa fields, 284,000 children work in abusive labor conditions for wages so low that many cocoa farmers cannot meet their family's basic needs.

THE INCONVENIENT TRUTH
Most flowers have been treated with pesticides. Send a pesticide-free bushel of flowers using Organic bouquet.com. They set high standards by using eco-friendly packaging with high certifications such as USDA Organic Certified, VeriFlora, Fair Trade, and more.

Mother Knows Best!
Looking for a greener rock for Valentine's Day? Blood diamonds be gone! Certified Conflict-Free diamonds are mined and produced under ethical conditions and not used toward war funds. Visit brilliantearth.com and greenkarat.com. They make unique styles from recycled metals and responsibly mined diamonds. At polarbeardiamond.com, they follow strict labor and environmental guidelines. For more info, visit conflictfreediamonds.org.

WEDDING INVITATIONS

Green It!

GROW-A-NOTE® CARDS / BLOOM® HANDMADE PAPER / GREENFIELD® WEDDING INVITATIONS/ ORGANIC WEDDING FAVORS

THE GOOD

Bloom and Grow-A-Note invites are embedded with wildflower seeds throughout the paper to recycle back into the ground! Greenfieldpaper .com wedding invitations and announcements are made with 100% natural and recycled content. Also look for 100% Post-Consumer Waste (PCW), 100% recycled or tree-free, FSC-certified paper and biodegradable inks.

THE GREEN

Paperless e-vites are the most eco-friendly way to go, and can be a great substitute for "Save the Date" announcements and thank you cards.

THE CONVENIENT TRUTH

Give your guests endangered species! The bite-size, all-natural chocolates give back to charitable organizations that support species, habitat, and humanity preservation efforts. Plus, they come in eco-friendly and biodegradable pouches.

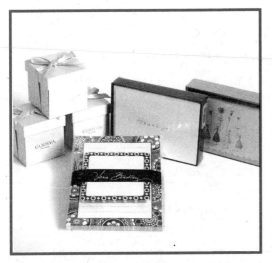

Skip It!

NON-ECO FRIENDLY INVITATIONS OR WEDDING FAVORS

THE UGLY

A Brides.com study reveals the average cost of a wedding is $28,082, and the average dress is $1,075.

Disposable invites add waste and pollution through production and consumption of precious trees.

THE INCONVENIENT TRUTH

Most wedding dresses are only worn for a few hours and can be quite costly. However you can buy or sell your gown at preownedwedding-dresses.com. They carry every price point including designer labels. Or, try www.bravobrides.com for new and pre-owned wedding items.

Sage Advice

The 4th "R" of green wedding efforts equals REGISTRY. Got enough household items to fill an entire landfill? Then you may want to look into charitable gift registries. JustGive.org allows you to create a page for guests to donate through the registry of your choice or make a gift in your name. The idofounda tion.org offers charitable invitations, donating 10% of each Carlson Craft invitation purchase to a charity.

BIRTHDAY PAPER

Green It!

RECYCLED BIRTHDAY WRAPPING PAPER / WRAPSACKS / BEESWAX BIRTHDAY CANDLES

THE GOOD

Go natural with the birthday candles by using hand dipped, 100% pure renewable beeswax candles. While burning, beeswax candles release negative ions, which actually eliminate impurities and allergens in the air.

THE GREEN

You've heard of re-gifting, but ever heard of re-carding? Reproducts (reproduct.net) greeting cards offer a program to send the card back in a postage paid method when finished, and they'll repurpose 100% of the card back into the backing of Shaw brand carpet.

THE CONVENIENT TRUTH

Reduce. Reuse. Pre-cycle? By choosing reusable gift bags such as Wrapsacks, you are actually pre-cycling, by saving trees and decreasing the over $5 billion worth of gift wrap sent to landfills every year.

Skip It!

NON-RECYCLED WRAPPING PAPER OR PARRAFIN BIRTHDAY CANDLES

THE UGLY

Most candles are made with a petro-leum by-product called paraffin.

THE INCONVENIENT TRUTH

It's always important to recycle your wrapping paper. However, each time paper is recycled, the fibers are broken down further, until they are too small to be reused and end up in the land-fills, so *reusing* is a better option.

Healthy Rx

If you must use wrapping paper, look for 100% recycled paper with soy based inks, such as fish lipspaperdesigns.com, which offers fun designer prints.

HALLOWEEN
Green It!

HOMEMADE COSTUME / NONTOXIC FACE PENCILS / ORGANIC TREATS

THE GOOD

Amazing Grass SuperFood drink powder is a delicious way to achieve daily serving of fruits and vegetables, in convenient packets for Halloween treats.

THE GREEN

Fear not! Serve Organic Spooky Smores bars. Or, the organic Endangered Species Bug Bites, where 10% of all net profits go to provide support to species, habitat, and humanity organizations. Learn more at chocolatebar.com

----

THE CONVENIENT TRUTH

Avoid toxic Halloween body paint and makeup. Healthier options like nontoxic face pencils are the best option.

Lisa's D.I.Y.

Green your Halloween by purchasing organic, healthy food for your child's Halloween party. Opt for real pumpkins. You can reuse the inside for roasted pumpkin seeds, soup, or pumpkin pie.

Skip It!
PLASTIC PACKAGING/ UNHEALTHY TREATS

THE UGLY
Conventional, non-organic cotton used to make outfits and costumes contains chemicals from synthetic pesticides.

THE INCONVENIENT TRUTH
Avoid the plastic pumpkin. Americans generate more than 10 million tons of plastic waste per year but only recycle 2% of it.

Healthy Rx
Don't want to hand out candy? Opt for alternatives like movie theater or DVD rental coupons, packets of seeds, or individual raisin boxes.

THANKSGIVING

Green It!

ORGANIC, FREE RANGE TURKEY / WHOLE GRAIN ROLLS

THE GOOD

Look for turkeys labeled USDA organic that meet specific requirements of organic farming.

THE GREEN

"Free-range" (regulated) indicates the turkey must have access to the outdoors, but it can be just a small fenced area. "Pasture raised" is a better choice, but it isn't regulated.

THE CONVENIENT TRUTH

A "good carb" contains "whole-grain" or "stone-ground" flour. Don't look for this on the outside of the package as they can stretch the truth here. Look for these words near the top of the ingredient list. They contain the entire grain kernel, hence more nutrients.

Remember just "wheat flour," and "unbleached wheat flour" are not the whole grain.

Sage Advice

Skinless turkey breast is one of Steve Pratt's fourteen SuperFoods! It made the list because it is the leanest protein on the planet. Turkey is also a good source of niacin, B6, and B12 which are needed for energy and a healthy heart, and is rich in zinc, which is important for the immune system and wound healing.

Skip It!

NONORGANIC TURKEY / WHITE FLOUR DINNER ROLLS

THE UGLY

Turkeys labeled "natural," "pastured," and "conventional meat" do not have the same standards or inspections as USDA Organic.

THE INCONVENIENT TRUTH

Rolls: Avoid the word enriched. It sounds nice, but its not. Enriched means they stripped the grain from everything good and healthy, including fiber and B vitamins, then attempted to add the vitamins back in, except the form they add back in is inferior and not absorbed as well by the body.

Sage Advice

Turkeys on factory farms are deprived of the simplest of pleasures, like running, building nests, spreading their wings, raising their young, and worse, are killed when they are only 5 or 6 months old. After their beaks and toes are burned off with a hot blade, they are crammed into grimy sheds. If you can't verify the source, opt for Tofurky, which is non-GMO and vegan. You can get PETA's free veggie starter kit here: www.goveg.com/order.asp.

EASTER

Green It!

DIVINE™ CHOCOLATE HAND-WOVEN BASKETS RAFFIA FOR GRASS / CERTIFIED ORGANIC CAGE-FREE EGGS

THE GOOD

All eggs are not created equal. USDA organic eggs come from farms using minimal amounts of pesticides, fungicides, herbicides, and commercial fertilizers, and are hormone free!

THE GREEN

Divine chocolate Brazil nuts are Fair Trade from Peru.

THE CONVENIENT TRUTH

Although no difference in taste, the white ear-lobed/white-feathered friends make white eggs, while red ear-lobed/dark-feathered hens make brown eggs.

Sage Advice

"Free-Range" eggs (regulated by USDA) means the hens have daily outdoor access, but no specified time or space is required.

"Cage-Free" eggs (not regulated by USDA) means the hens are not confined to cages, but may or may not have had access to the outdoors.

"Pasture-raised" eggs (not USDA regulated) indicates the hens eat feed from pastures, but might not roam free.

Skip It!

PLASTIC EASTER BASKET AND ARTIFICIAL GRASS / NONORGANIC CHOCOLATE / NONORGANIC EGGS

THE UGLY

Plastic Easter baskets and grass contribute to pollution in production and use limited resources. Look for handmade, wooden, or ceramic baskets and raffia instead of plastic grass.

THE INCONVENIENT TRUTH

Even labels on eggs that sound good can still come from farms with inhumane treatment. Visit humanefacts.org or peta.org to learn more.

Healthy Rx

Divine chocolate Easter eggs are great for vegans and vegetarians. They contain no artificial flavorings, colorings, preservatives, milk, milk derivatives, wheat, or wheat derivatives, and are gluten free.

CHAPTER 9

EXTREME GREEN

YOU KNOW YOU'RE EXTREME when you:

1. Use menstrual cups and reusable pads vs. conventional tampons & pads (Playtex, Kotex)

Conventional cotton is one of the most pesticide intensive crops there is. If you're buying tampons made from this type of cotton, you may be exposing yourself to the chemical residues from those pesticides as well as chlorine from the bleaching process to whiten. Go greener by choosing reusable menstrual cups and pads instead of traditional tampons or pads.

Unlike the original menstrual cup of the 1930's made of latex, the Diva Cup is reusable and made from silicone, which is latex-free, plastic-free and BPA-free! One menstrual cup can last you up to a year, which saves you money and reduces the billions of tons of disposable waste that is dumped into landfills each year.

Look for The Diva Cup (www.divacup.com). Or try The Keeper (made of natural gum rubber and lasts up to 10 years) or The Moon Cup (made of silicone), which can both be found at www.keeper.com. For those who prefer the greenest of pads, try Glad Rags (www.glad rags.com), which are organic cotton reusable day pads that offer a healthy alternative to disposables. They really save green since each pad lasts five years. One stop shopping for all of the above is available at www.goddesspads.com

Or, if this is all a bit too much for your time-of-the-month green threshold, then opt at a minimum for chlorine free and organic tampons and pads. These are offered by Natracare and Seventh Generation and found at most health food stores. Organic cotton is safer for you, for farmers and for our environment. If just one out of every 20 women switched to organic tampons, we could reduce pesticide use by 750,000 pounds a year.

2. Use vegetable oil, not gas for vehicle

Does the dependency on foreign oil make you cringe? You are not alone. If you already drive a diesel car or are in the market for one, consider running it on vegetable oil instead. Unlike diesel or regular gas, vegetable oil is a renewable resource, and it's biodegradable. You will help reduce petroleum consumption. And, since vegetable oil runs cleaner by emitting less CO_2 into the air, you will be contributing far less pollution.

Be aware that only diesel cars can be converted to run on veggie oil as these engines work by heating the vegetable oil.

Converting a vehicle can be an affordable option for the do-it-yourselfer with kits starting as low as $595. You can also purchase kits in the range of $1K to $3K at Greasecar.com, which allow you to run the car on SVO – straight vegetable oil. Not to be confused with biodiesel, which requires the vegetable oil go through a process called transesterification, SVO utilizes 100% vegetable oil and requires a modification to the engine only.

Or, try Frybrid.com, which offers a Diesel/Vegetable oil hybrid technology. There are even classes available to teach you the proper process to convert. Offered by The Yestermorrow Design/Build School, the "Biofuels" workshop can be found at: www.yestermorrow.org

Once the conversion is complete, the savings begin. Many restaurants must pay a fee to dispose of their fryer oil; therefore, they will gladly donate their used portions. After filtering, the oil can then be used to run converted vehicles. Note: the EPA has not registered these oils as legal use in vehicles due to lack of emission research.

3. Use Solar Home Heliostats; not electricity

As long as you don't mind adding a bunch of pole-mounted mirrors to your backyard landscaping, Solar Home Heliostats (www.practicalsolar.com) are a great green way to reduce your utility bill and solve a variety of common household problems without wasting energy. Easy to install, the mirrors track the sun and focus the energy they capture wherever it best serves you utilizing your own computer to run. All day long, you can light an otherwise dark room, heat a chilly space, provide more sunshine to your garden, direct light to a shaded solar panel and even quickly dry a line of wet clothes. The mirrors create 3,000 times the energy they consume, and there is little risk of fire or blindness even when they focus the sunlight into your home through your windows.

If you're not ready to commit to this avant-garde backyard installation, start small by replacing your electricity sucking docking station with a Kinesis K3 Wind and Solar Charger (www.kinesisindustries.com). This much smaller and less attention-grabbing device enables you to harvest the wind and sunlight to charge your cell phone, mp3, GPS, earpiece, camera and gaming devices.

4. Use the Bag-E-Wash™ & Dryer; not new plastic baggies

Plastic bags are everywhere—not just in packaging and at the supermarket checkout, but also on the beach and in the ocean, by the side of the road and in landfills by the ton. In fact, the U.S. produces 10 pounds of plastic bags per person *every year*. Most get used once and tossed. Clearly the greenest strategy is to stop using plastic bags. However, as noble as this sounds, it's a hard one to put into practice in day-to-day life. What about the kids' lunches or snacks for the hike? What about toiletries in your carry-on bag? The list goes on.

A more realistic strategy is to reduce your use of plastic bags wherever possible, and wash and reuse the plastic bags you do need. The Bag-E-Wash (www.bag-e-wash.com) is dishwasher safe and the company estimates one box of 30 gallon-size bags washed with Bag-E-Wash™ and reused 50 times each saves $150.00 and keeps 1,500 bags out of the landfills. The Bag Dryer helps by providing an easy place to hang up to 8 washed bags so they dry completely with no mess. The dryer itself is made from sustainable wood with a non-toxic finish and it looks a lot neater than having your drying bags strewn around your kitchen.

5. Use Poo Poo paper products; not virgin paper

First there was recycling and re-gifting; now there's poo-cycling and poo-gifting! The Great Elephant Poo Poo Paper Company has an online poo-tique at www.Poopoopaper.com! The company manufactures 100% recycled and odorless paper products made from our fiber-eating animal friends' poo, including elephant, cow, panda, and horse to create a wide variety of products: paper, journals, notebooks, greeting cards, wine bags, and even a bouquet of roses! You can frame your loved one in the poo picture frame (or an ex should you find this more suitable). The poo, or dung, is thoroughly cleaned and additional plant fibers are added back in to add strength. With over 150 unique items, you don't have to sacrifice choices because *the poo's the limit.*

6. Use the MOTO™ W233 recycled cell phone; not a regular cell phone

Speak responsibly! And we don't just mean when driving. When choosing a cell phone or PDA, look beyond the bells and whistles and into where your hard-earned dollars are going, and where they'll end up. Is the phone or the manufacturer taking steps toward social responsibility in the production of the phone? If not, you may want to consider a phone made with recycled plastic water bottles like the MOTO W233 Renew, the first certified Carbonfree cell phone with up to nine hours of talk time. Even the plastic housing is 100% recyclable and can be sent back in their postage paid envelope. Visit www.motorola.com. Remember, with any cell phone, to look a step further beyond green packaging and consider the radiation emitted from the phone. If you are not sure, just enter the name of your phone in the EWG database at: ewg.org/cellphone-radiation to find out where yours ranks.

A green round of applause for the Samsung Impression and the Motorola RAZR V8 for being the two lowest in radiation based on EWG's report Cell Phone Radiation: *Science Review on Cancer Risks and Children's Health.*

BONUS: FOUR "TOP 10" LISTS!

TOP 10 STEPS TO A GREENER OFFICE

R EPORTS ESTIMATE 69 MILLION workers miss days of work due to illness. In fact, together, they miss *407 million workdays,* and that translates to $48 billion in lost economic output each year. Studies show that one of the major culprits causing all these lost workdays and money is the workplace itself. Unhealthy air and toxic chemicals abound in the typical office, and it's literally making workers sick. Here are a few easy steps can help you create a healthier and greener office.

1. Conserve Energy

According to the Department of Energy, office buildings account for nearly 30% of commercial energy demand. Yet even a simple change like using your computer's sleep mode can dramatically decrease office energy use. Sleep mode uses very little power because it stores the documents you've been using in memory, and the monitor goes black. Since 40% of the energy it takes to run your computer goes to the monitor, using the sleep mode regularly can add up to a big savings.

2. Defeat Dust

Dust is the second leading cause of allergies, followed by pollen. Left to linger, dust gives toxins from cleaning and office supplies and electronics a place to land. In fact, a 2005 study conducted by 9 environmental organizations titled *Sick of Dust*, found chemicals used in computers, cosmetics, upholstery, pesticides, and other products present in dust. Although the chemicals are considered toxic or harmful to the immune and reproductive systems, they are legal. That means, the more dust around, the more you are exposed to these toxins, thereby polluting you indoor air. On top of that, many offices have a very serious dust mite problem, and there are likely millions in yours. Each dust ball can contain as many as 250,000 mites. To stop being so hospitable to the mites and rid your office of other contaminants, use an air purifier (page 84) that features a true-medical grade HEPA in combination with military carbon cloth or granular carbon filter which will aid in the absorption of toxic chemicals that may be emanating from office equipment like the printer and fax.

3. Create a Green Sanctuary

Many plants like Gerber daises, philodendrons, and peace lilies absorb airborne pollutants, making the air you breathe cleaner. Although plants are not a replacement for an air purifier, they do a great job of filtering out various contaminants that are emitted into the air by office furniture, carpeting, electronics, and office supplies. Because they absorb these contaminants through their leaves, it's important to dust the leaves regularly.

4. What's Outside Your Drinking Water?

Over 1 million plastic bottles go into landfills every day in America. These require 1.5 million barrels of oil to produce, and more than 1 million tons of plastic that emits more greenhouse gas than 500,000 cars. The wrong bottle can expose you to chemicals that pose some serious health risks. Check the number under the bottle inside the triangle. Use only plastic bottles that are numbered #1, #2, #4 and #5. They contain polyethylene or polypropylene, which have the least toxic additives. These plastics are also non-chlorinated, which is good for your health as well as the environment. Avoid bottles that are made from PVC (#3), polystyrene (#6), and polycarbonate (#7), which contain hormone disruptors and other potential health threats.

5. See the Light

More than 25% of all office energy use comes from artificial lighting. Reduce office electric bills by using Light-Emitting Diode (LED) bulbs, instead of the more popular compact fluorescent (CFLs), fluorescent, or incandescent bulbs. LEDs are now the cutting-edge of green light bulbs. They are actually brighter and more energy efficient than CFLs.

6. Conserve Paper

Paper makes up 40% of all our garbage and that is more than any other type of waste. The average employee uses 10,000 sheets of paper a year for printed proposals, emails, and other documents. This is bad news when you consider the paper-making process causes deforestation, water pollution, and demolishes habitats of thousands of animals. Buying recycled paper is more important than ever. Look for post-consumer recycled content paper that does not rely on newly cut trees. Also, go digital as much as possible and make sure you only print what is absolutely necessary. You can pay your office bills online, and most people are

content to receive and forward electronic documents.

7. Avoid "Electromagnetic Pollution"

Studies show that the electronics you have in your office can lead to serious health concerns, including increased stress levels. The popularity of wireless laptops, a wireless keyboard, wireless mouse, and cell phones are making matters worse. As a result, many people are literally becoming ill from the 21st-century office. To protect yourself, use cable modems whenever possible and air tube wireless headsets during cell phone use.

8. Use Eco-Friendly Cleaners

The National Research Council estimates that fewer than 30% of the roughly 17,000 petrochemicals available for use have been tested for their effects on human and environmental health. That is why it is important to use healthy, organic cleaning products. Recommend to your facility manager that he or she hire cleaning companies that use healthy cleaners. If this can't be changed, at least make sure you're wiping down your own workspace with eco-friendly, healthier, all-purpose cleaners (page 50).

9. Beware of the Office Break Room

Far too often people stand around and watch their food cook in the microwave. By doing this, you unknowingly subject yourself to harmful microwaves. Make sure to be at least six feet away from the microwave when it is in use. Also another concern is unfiltered water from the kitchen sink. Tap water is poorly regulated, and most water public utilities test for only on average 100 chemicals out of potentially *thousands* that can be present. Convince your office manager to invest in a reverse osmosis or carbon-based water filter. This will provide you with better drinking water and a better source for cleaning fruit you bring to the office.

10. Don't Trash It

When throwing out old office electronics, make sure to dispose of it in the proper manner. In many states in the U.S., it is illegal to throw out old electronics, and you may even be fined. Look for community recycling events or local drop off stations that will recycle and reuse salvageable materials. In addition to electronics, make sure you properly dispose of your printer's ink cartridges. They can take up to 450 years to decompose. Recycle your old ones, and next time you buy, go with refilable cartridges, which cost up to 75% less than new ones.

TOP 10 STEPS
TO A HEALTHY NURSERY

AVOIDING TOXIC MATERIALS IN the nursery is becoming a top priority for new parents. Creating a green nursery just makes sense, since your delicate little one will spend up to 17 hours a day in there! Consider everything your baby comes in contact with and choose your nursery furnishings with natural, organic materials in mind.

1. Use Nontoxic Paints and Finishes

Before baby comes home from the hospital, you can start preparing your green nursery. Babies are particularly vulnerable to the dangers of Volatile Organic Compounds (VOCs) found in common commercial oil and water-based paints. Your safest bet to avoid or reduce these residual toxins is to choose "Zero VOC" or "Low VOC" paints and finishes (page 88). As a rule, painting should be completed at least a month before the baby arrives, and, because VOCs are also harmful to fetuses, it should be done by someone other than a pregnant mom.

2. Choose Safe Flooring

Although carpeting can help create the soft, quiet space you want for your nursery, it can also expose your baby to harmful toxins. The chemicals in the carpet backing, adhesives, and the fibers themselves, as well as the stain or water-resistant treatments that have been applied to the carpet, can all emit VOCs and other pollutants. You can be sure your baby will spend a lot of time on the floor so stay away from new synthetic carpeting. Instead choose natural and hard surfaced flooring like wood (with a low VOC sealant), linoleum, or cork (page 78). Hard surfacing is easier to maintain and less likely to trap potential contaminants than wall-to-wall carpeting. If an area rug is needed, be sure to choose natural fibers and untreated options.

3. Go for Real Wood Over Particleboard

The crib is your baby's "home" and needs to be as pure as possible in every way. You may save a few bucks by buying particleboard furniture for the nursery, but your baby's long-term health is worth spending more. Like toxic paint and carpeting, these products also offgas VOCs such as carcinogenic formaldehyde. Look for solid wood products that are finished without toxins. If you can't be sure on the finish, it's a good idea to buy an unfinished crib and finish it yourself with a zero VOC product.

4. Buy a Natural Crib Mattress

Conventional crib mattresses are infused with toxic fire retardants and antibacterial pesticides. They are also stuffed and covered in petroleum-based materials. All of this means, that when your baby takes those long naps you've been hoping for or finally sleeps through the night, you won't be resting easy knowing what she's breathing as she sleeps. Instead, choose an organic mattress that is free of these dangerous chemicals like The Green Nest organic crib mattresses with a real wool moisture pad (page 148). These are made with certified wool, which is a natural fire retardant, as well as non-toxic natural rubber and organic cotton.

5. Choose Organic Baby Clothes and Bedding

Conventional cotton is not good for the environment because of all the pesticides that go into it. Once it's turned into bedding or clothes it is treated with more harsh chemicals to prevent wrinkling, bacteria, or fire. Choose certified organic cotton that's untreated, unbleached, and unprocessed for bed sheets and baby clothes. Also make sure that colored dyes in the fabric have all-natural ingredients derived from nature's plants and minerals.

6. Surround Your Baby with Natural Toys

In 2007, 12 million children's toys were recalled, but even the ones that haven't been recalled can be unhealthy. Many of these toys are made of plastic, which is a major contributor to indoor air pollution. Plastic toys, such as teething rings and even pacifiers, can expose your baby to toxins that have been shown to harm kids' hormonal systems and reproductive development. Be especially wary of imported toys from China, which may contain lead, which is a neurotoxin. There are many natural cloth and solid wood toys available on the Internet. Choose quality over quantity and look for options that can be handed down through the generations instead of tossed in the landfill when they are outgrown.

7. Use Safe Baby Bottles

Bisphenol A (BPA) is a hormone-disrupting chemical considered to be potentially harmful to human health and the environment that is found in common plastic baby bottles. Studies have shown that very low levels of Bisphenol A in a baby can cause behavioral problems like hyperactivity and impaired learning. It's especially important to get rid of scratched and worn polycarbonate feeding bottles, which are most likely to leach Bisphenol-A into liquids. Choose BPA-free plastic baby bottles or glass bottles for feeding your baby.

8. Use Nontoxic Baby-Care Products

Baby's personal care products can contain toxins that are known to cause long-term health problems. Some of the worst offenders are fragrance, dyes, preservatives, and antibacterials. To find greener baby-care products, look for products that disclose all of their ingredients on the label. You can research specific products by brand on the Environmental Working Group's Skin Deep website (www.cosmeticsdata base.com), where you will find information on ingredients and how the product ranks in terms of toxins.

9. Filter Baby's Bath Water

Chlorine can be an immediate problem for kids with asthma, but it has also been linked to more long-term health problems including breast cancer. When the water becomes steam or the chlorine comes in contact with other chemicals in your bathroom, it can release even more dangerous toxins into the air you're breathing. Making matters worse, your baby's skin is 5 times thinner than yours, which means he is absorbing much more than you are into his little body. To reduce breathing and absorbing all this chlorine, use a bath filter like the Bath Ball Tub Filter or Baby Shower Filter found at greennest.com. The baby's bath will be healthier and cleaner, and his skin will be even softer without the drying effects of chlorine.

10. Use Nontoxic Cleaning and Pest Control Products

Once you've created your green nursery, you will want to keep it clean and keep the dust mites at bay. However, it's important to use nontoxic cleaning products, so you don't wind up polluting the air as you "clean." An easy and inexpensive mixture of water and white distilled vinegar in a spray bottle is all you need to clean and disinfect every surface in your nursery, including the windows! You can even soak bath toys in vinegar and water to clean and fight mold. Wash your baby's bedding and clothes in a nontoxic, fragrance-free mild detergent and use non-toxic pest control products that can control the pests while keeping your baby's air clean.

TOP 10 STEPS
TO A HEALTHY BEDROOM

NOT GETTING ENOUGH ZZZS? Feeling less than rested in the morning? Take a look around your bedroom and you might discover that you don't have a sleeping disorder, but rather a room that's not restful. If sleep continually eludes you, it's time to evaluate your surroundings and take some steps to create a true sleep sanctuary.

1. De-clutter Your Room

Clutter traps dust and dust can trigger a host of allergies. If your room is full of books, newspapers and knick-knacks clean it up and clear it out. If you keep a computer in the bedroom—move it! Ditto for hobby supplies. Computers contain cadmium, lead, flame retardants, epoxy plastics. Hobby supplies contribute toxic inks and glues. You want to avoid breathing in these dangerous toxins at night.

2. Remove the Carpet and Use Area Rugs

Rugs can make a room cozier, but they also can harbor toxins, bacteria, and even bugs. Toxic chemicals can be found in carpet backing, adhesives, and the fibers themselves, as well as stain or water resistant treatments that have been applied to the carpet. If you can't live without carpet in your bedroom get an area rug or have a piece of carpet cut to the size of the room, air it out, and wash and rinse it with water before having it fitted. Make sure to choose untreated, natural fiber options (page 76).

3. Choose an Organic Mattress and Linens

When it comes to selecting a mattress that will give you a good night's sleep, it's even more important to consider what's in the mattress than to test how it feels. Most mattresses are loaded with chemicals including toxic flame retardants and pesticides. The most common flame retardants (PBDEs) are also Persistent Organic Pollutants (POPs) that are suspected to cause damage to reproductive and nervous systems and delay development in children. Luckily greener mattresses are becoming more widely available. Look for options made from organic cotton, natural latex, or naturally fire-retardant wool. Replace old bedding, and especially sheets that are chemically treated to be "wrinkle-free," with organic linens. And use organic barrier covers for pillows and mattresses to provide an allergen barrier.

4. Check the Room for Mold

Mold can wreak havoc on your health from mild allergy-like symptoms to debilitating illness, depending on the level of mold in a building and the sensitivity of the exposed individuals. Mold can grow on a variety of surfaces like drywall and wood as long as there is moisture to feed it. If there's a leak in a roof, window or plumbing, mold can even grow unseen behind walls and under floors. If you suspect mold, contact a remediation specialist in your area to have the problem corrected immediately.

5. Air Out Dry Cleaning

An abundance of unhealthy chemicals are used in the dry cleaning process. To make matters worse, we wrap our dry-cleaning in plastic and leave it in our closets where it can offgas those toxins for months. But you can lessen your exposure. Before you bring your dry cleaned clothes into your bedroom, air them out for 3 to 4 days and choose a green-friendly dry cleaner (page 58).

6. Use Battery Powered Alarm Clocks

Research has shown that exposure to high magnetic fields while sleeping can cause severe long-term illness. Many electric clocks produce high magnetic fields. Replace your alarm clock with a rechargable battery-powered model.

7. Turn Off Circuit Breakers Before Bedtime.

Electric fields affect the body's bio-communication system, keeping you from sleeping soundly. Even with everything unplugged, current still runs through the walls and floors of your bedroom. Turn off the circuit breaker to your bedroom when you turn in at night, leaving important breakers on such as those running your refrigerator on. You can also use Automatic Demand Switches which can be professionally installed by an electrician. These are set to turn off automatically only the selected breakers affecting your sleeping area as soon as the last light is turned out. These are convenient because they automatically turn the power back on when you turn the lights, or selected switch, on again, never leaving you in the dark.

8. Eliminate or Shield from Radio Frequency Signals

Radio frequency (RF) signals from portable phones, cell phones, and wireless devices have been shown to interfere with the body's immune system. Turn them off before going to bed or keep them a safe distance (6 feet or more) from your bed while sleeping.

9. Avoid Metal Beds

Metal frames and metal box springs can amplify and distort the earth's natural magnetic field, which can lead to a non-restful sleep. Use natural materials instead. By choosing a natural latex organic mattress, you will avoid any metal springs in your mattress. Furniture can also make a significant contribution to the chemical concoction in bedroom air. Choose solid wood furniture with nontoxic finishes. Avoid particleboard, which can emit toxic Volatile Organic Compounds such as formaldehyde used in the resins.

10. Create Healthy Indoor Air

Since we spend a third of our life in our bedrooms, it is vital to maintain clean and healthy air—in this room in particular. Make sure to use an air purifier with a filter that has HEPA filtration as well as a blend of carbon and zeolite like Healthmate at Green Nest for removal of biological and chemical contaminants. Don't forget to change your HVAC furnace air filters regularly—every 3 months to be safe (page 82).

TOP 10 GREEN CAREERS FOR THE FUTURE

IF THE FORECASTERS HAVE IT RIGHT, the "green-collar" economy is the one that's about to take off. This is the sector of the economy focused on sustainability and turning back the tides of global warming and other environmental crises. It's clear that now's the time to green your resume. Besides using recycled paper, lead with your values to make a sustainable career change.

1. Farmer

Two factors make farming a great, green career choice. First, America's farmers are aging and will be looking to retire over the next decade. Second, to achieve more sustainable agriculture, we'll need more farmers than ever. The days of the mega-farm and its dependence on petroleum based fertilizers and tractors are numbered, as the toll they take on the environment has become painfully apparent. Instead, we need lots of small, organic farms to meet the demand for food without sacrificing the environment.

2. Forester

The World Bank reports there are 1.6 billion people on the planet who depend on the forests for their livelihood. As the forests shrink and the competition for them intensifies, there is a growing need for green professionals to serve as stewards, and educate us all on how to use the forests in environmentally and socially sound ways.

3. Solar Power Installer

Innovation and eco-friendly tax credits are making solar power a more affordable option for homes and commercial buildings alike. That means the future looks bright for solar power installers. Currently, the industry employs around 25,000 to 35,000 workers in the United States. According to the Solar Energy Industries Association, that number will quadruple by 2016.

4. Energy Efficiency Builder

According to Ezra Drissman of *Green Careers Guide*, the green building industry will create 2 million new green jobs in the near future. That's not just because demand is increasing, but the government is expected to invest heavily in this industry. The necessary skill sets run the gamut from roofing, skylight, and window installation to engineering and architectural design.

5. Wind Turbine Fabricator

If you have skills working with metal, wind turbines may be a great fit for you. Wind blows away the competition in the world of alternative energy with some 60,000 workers in the U.S. alone. This number is set to grow as we look for more ways to curb our dependence on oil.

6. Conservation Biologist

Opportunities abound for those who have the background and desire to teach and/or research ways to preserve the earth's ecosystems. This is another area where government funding is starting to pour in, and government agencies, nonprofits, and private businesses are looking for qualified candidates.

7. Green MBA and Entrepreneur

From start-ups with the hottest new eco-friendly idea to established companies making the switch to going green, all types of business professionals with green values and knowledge are needed.

8. Recycler

There are already over 1 million recycling jobs in the United States with more than 200,000 of those in the fastest growing area of the recycling industry, secondary-steel production. Recycled steel continues to make as much sense from a business standpoint as it does from an environmental one, and it may be your best bet if you want to get involved.

9. Sustainability Systems Developer

As we shift to using more alternative energy, the need grows for technological workers who can help plan, create, and manage the networks and grids that will keep it all going. According to Fast Company, the most in-demand will be coders who are experienced with massive enterprise resource planning and developers who are experts in open source and web 2.0 applications.

10. Urban Planner

Green urban planners don't think about quaint commuter neighborhoods with single-family, multi-car garages. They think mass transit, bicycle lanes, and work/live communities. But they also have to be planning for possible environmental disasters such as floods and heat waves and how to manage garbage. According to Fast Company, experts predict green urban planning jobs mostly in local government offices will grow 15% by 2016. Source: *Fast Company*, "Ten Best Green Jobs for the Next Decade."

ACKNOWLEDGMENTS

WE WOULD LIKE TO THANK THE NUMEROUS COMPANIES, both large and small who go above and beyond to make their products healthy and safe for both people and planet. From the mom and pops up to fortune 50 companies, efforts are being made and we've taken notice. We'd also like to thank the companies who were overlooked in this book. We did our very best to include you, but it would be impossible to mention everyone. A resource section has been added in the rear of the book to include additional companies that should be acknowledged and supported. Visit www.JustGreenIt.net for updates to this guide.

We would wish to thank our parents, friends, and family for their undying support along our green journey. Special thanks to Geoffrey Stone at Running Press and Holly Schmidt, Allan Penn, Lisa Clancy, Justine Power, Nicole Valencia, and Chris Bird. Thank you all for your hard work and dedication!

ABBREVIATIONS

AAA – American Automobile Association

ACEEE – American Council for an Energy-Efficient Economy is a nonprofit devoted to research, publications, and conferences on energy efficiency in buildings, utilities, applicances, office equipment, industry, and transportation.

ALA – American Lung Association

ALS – Ammonium Lauryl Sulfate is a mild foaming agent used in shampoos and cleansers.

APEs – Alkylphenol Ethoxylates are a group of hormone-disrupting compounds found in detergents.

BBP – Butyl Benzyl Phthalate is used as a plasticizer for polyvinyl chloride in vinyl flooring.

BFRs – Brominated Flame Retardants are chemicals used in various products including electronics.

BPA – Bisphenol A is a hormone-disrupting chemical considered to be potentially harmful to human health and the environment that is found in common plastic baby bottles.

PCW – Postconsumer Waste

CFCs – Chlorofluorocarbons are a family of non-reactive, nonflamable gases and volatile liquids.

CFLs – Compact Fluorescent bulbs are a type of fluorescent lamp that uses less electricity than incandescent bulbs but contains mercury that is toxic to the environment.

CO$_2$ – Carbon Dioxide

CRI – Carpet and Rug Institute is the trade association representing manufacturers and suppliers of carpets, rugs, and floor covering.

CPSC – Consumer Product Safety Commission is a government agency charged with protecting the public from unreasonable risks of serious injury or death from thousands of types of consumer products.

DBP – Dibutyl Phthalate is a harmful organic compound used to help make plastics soft and flexible.

DEA – Diethanolamine is a harmful chemical that is used as a wetting agent in shampoos.

DEHP – di (2-ethylhexyl) phthalate is a harmful organic compound found in many plastics.

EFAs – Essential Fatty Acids are necessary fats that the human body cannot generate and are found in many types of fish.

EMF – Electromagnetic Field

EPA – Environmental Protection Agency is a government agency whose mission is to protect human health and safeguard the natural environment.

EPS – Expanded Polystyrene or Styrofoam

EWG – Environmental Working Group is an environmental organization that works to protect children from toxic chemicals.

FSC – Forest Stewardship Council (FSC) is a nonprofit organization devoted to encouraging the responsible management of the world's forests.

FDA – Food and Drug Administration is the federal agency responsible for regulating the safety of foods, dietary supplements, drugs vaccines, biological medical products, blood products, medical devices, radiation-emitting devices, veterinary products, and cosmetics.

GMO – Genetically Modification Organism are organisms whose genetic makeup has been altered using genetic engineering.

GRAS – Generally Regarded As Safe

HDPE – High-Density Polyethylene is a harmful type of plastic (#2) polyvinyl chloride (V, PVC – vinyl plastic)

HEPA FILTERS – High Efficiency Particulate Air filters are fibrous air filters that remove at least 99.97% of airborne particles 0.3 micrometers in diameter.

LCA – Life Cycle Analysis is a scientific method to record people's environmental impact throughout their entire lives.

LDPE – Low-Density Polyethylene is a harmful type of plastic (#4).

LEDs – Light Emitting Diode is an electronic light source that is more efficient and produces less heat than incandescent bulbs.

LEED – Leadership in Energy and Environmental Design is an accreditation of hotels by the U.S. Green Building Council.

MEA – Monoethanolamine is a harmful chemical that is used as a wetting agent in shampoos.

NOP – National Organic Program is the federal regulatory framework governing organic food.

NPEs – Nonylphenol Ethoxylates is a synthesized organic compound used in laundry detergents and is harmful to human hormones.

PAN – Pesticide Action Network

PBDEs – Polybrominated diphenylethers are a particular class of toxic flame retardant chemicals.

PCW – Post-Consumer Waste

PFCs – Perflourochemicals are chemicals used to coat nonstick cookware.

PFCs – Perfluorinated compounds are persistent organic pollutants that are used to make materials stain and water resistent.

PET, PETE – Polyethylene Terephthalate is a toxic thermoplastic resin used for food and beverage containers.

POPs – Persistent Organic Pollutants are a particular class of toxic flame retardant chemicals.

PP – Polypropylene is a toxic thermoplastic polymer used for packaging materials and stationary.

PS – Polystyrene is a toxic thermoplastic polymer used for various packages and containers.

rBGH – Recombinant Bovine Growth Hormone is a synthesized protein hormone given to cattle.

REC –Renewable Energy Certificate represent environmental attributes of power produced from renewable energy projects, and they allow you the flexibility not to have to switch electricity suppliers.

RF – Radio Frequency

SEI – Solar Energy International is a USA nonprofit that helps others use renewable energy and environmental building technologies through education.

SLES – Sodium Laureth Sulphate is a mild foaming agent commonly used in shampoos and cleansers.

SLS – Sodium Lauryl Sulfate is an anionic surfactant used in many cleaning products.

TEA – Triethanolamine is a harmful chemical that is used as a wetting agent in shampoos.

THM – Trihalomethane is a chemical compound used as solvants or regrigerants and are used in drinking water purification.

TSCA – Federal Toxic Substances Control Act of 1976 is an act of Congress that limits the power of the EPA and allows chemicals into the market with little to no testing.

USDA – The U.S. Department of Agriculture a federal agency that oversees the agriculture sector.

VCS – Voluntary Carbon Standard is a global benchmark standard for voluntary, project-based, greenhouse gas emission reductions, and removals.

VOCs – Volatile Organic Compounds are emitted as gases from certain solids or liquids, which may have short- and long-term adverse health effects.

GREEN RESOURCES

This resource list provides Web addresses for many of the green products mentioned in this book. Look for a comprehensive list and any updates online at www.JustGreenIt.net.

AIR FRESHENER
- Young Living Diffuser (www.youngliving.org/greennest)

AIR PURIFIERS
- 3M Filtrete Ultra Clean Air Purifier (www.3m.com/product)
- Lowe's Idylis Air Purifier (www.idylishome.com)
- Healthmate HM-400 Air Purifier by Austin Air (www.austinair.com)
- IQ Air Purifier (www.iqair.com)

Note: In order of price-point and square footage covered (lowest to highest)

BABY FOOD
- Happy Baby Organic (www.happybabyfood.com)
- O Organics (www.carrsqc.com)
- Plum Organics Frozen (www.plumorganics.com)

BABY POWDER
- Baby Organic Coconut Baby Powder (www.bodysenseshop.com)

- JASCO Organics Velvet Natural Baby Powder (www.jascoorganics.com)

BATTERIES
- Green Batteries (www.greenbatteries.com)

BBQ CLEANER
- Simple Green BBQ Cleaner (www.simplegreen.com)

BED SHEETS
- Coyuchi Organic Sheets (www.coyuchi.com)

BEVERAGES
- IZZE (www.izze.com)
- Steaz Energy Drink (www.steazenergy.com)

BIRTHDAY CANDLES, CARDS, PAPER
- Beeswax Birthday Candles (www.bigdipperwaxworks.com)
- Reproduct (www.reproduct.net)
- 100% Recycled Paper with Soy Based Inks (www.fishlipspaperdesigns.com)
- Wrapsacks (www.wrapsacks.com)

BLEACH

- 20 Mule Team Borax (www.20muleteamlaundry.com)
- Ecover Non Chlorine Bleach (www.ecover.com)
- Seventh Generation Chlorine Free Bleach (www.seventhgeneration.com)

BODY CARE

- Aubrey Organics Rosa Mosqueta Moisturizing Cleansing Bar (www.aubrey-organics.com)
- Desert Essence Jojoba Oil for Hair, Skin, and Scalp (www.desertessence.com)
- Pangea Organics Bar Soaps (pangeaorganics-store.sparkart.net)
- Perfect Organics (www.perfectorganics.com)

BUILDING PROJECT

- Vail Green Home – Trisa and Ryan Sutter's sustainable home building project (www.vailgreenhome.com)

CANDLES

- Green Nest Soy Candle (www.greennest.com)

CAR RENTAL – HYBRID/LOW EMISSION

- Green Travel Hub by Rezhub.Com (www.rezhub.com/GreenTravel)

CARBON OFFSET COMPANIES

- Carbon Fund (www.carbonfund.org)
- Native Energy (www.nativeenergy.com)
- Terra Pass (www.terrapass.com)

CARS – VEGETABLE FUEL SYSTEMS

- Diesel/Vegetable Oil Hybrid Technology (www.Frybrid.com)
- Greasecar Vegetable Fuel Systems (www.Greasecar.com)

CARWASH – WATERLESS

- Freedom Waterless Car Wash (www.freedomwaterlesscarwash.com)
- Lucky Earth Waterless (www.luckyearth.com)

CAULKING

- AFM Safecoat Caulking Compound (www.afmsafecoat.com)

CELL PHONE – ECO FRIENDLY

- Moto W233 Renew (www.motorola.com)
- Air Tube Headset (www.greennest.com)

CHRISTMAS TREE RECYCLING

- Earth 911 (www.Earth911.org)

CLEANING

- Baking Soda (www.armhammer.com)
- Bon Ami (www.bonami.com)
- Clean Home Green Home (www.amazon.com)
- Eco-Me Home Kit (www.eco-me.com)

- Green Nest All-Purpose Cleaner (www.greennest.com)
- Green Works Dish Soap (www.greenworkscleaners.com)
- Method All-Purpose Cleaner (www.methodhome.com)
- Mrs. Meyers All-Purpose Cleaner (www.mrsmeyers.com)
- Seventh Generation Free and Clear (www.seventhgeneration.com)

COFFEE

- 365 Whole Foods (www.wholefoodsmarket.com)
- Green Mountain Roasters (www.greenmountaincoffee.com)
- Grounds for Change (www.groundsforchange.com)
- Newman's Own Organic (www.newmansownorganics.com)
- O Organics (www.carrsqc.com)
- Teccino (www.teeccino.com)

COOKIES

- Newman's Own Organic (www.newmansownorganics.com)
- O Organics (www.carrsqc.com)

COOKWARE

- Chantal (www.chantal.com)
- Cuisinart Greengourmet 12-Piece Cookware Set (www.cuisinart.com)
- Le Creuset Grill Pan (www.williams-sonoma.com)
- Lodge Muffin Pan (www.lodgemfg.com)
- Williams Sonoma – Emile Henry Artisan Loaf Pan (www.williams-sonoma.com)

COFFEE CUPS

- I Am Not A Paper Cup (www.dcigift.com)
- Starbucks To Go Cold Cup (www.starbucksstore.com)

CUTLERY AND DINNERWARE

- Bare by Solo (www.barebysolo.com)
- Cutlery & Containers – reusable (To-Go Ware (www.to-goware.com)
- Preserve Cutlery (www.preserveproducts.com)

DAIRY

- Organic Valley Organic Milk & Yogurt (www.organicvalley.coop)
- Stoneyfield Farm Organic Milk & Yogurt (www.stonyfield.com)

DEODORANT

- B+Drier Antiperspirant (www.cosmeticsdatabase.com)
- Lafe's Natural Deodorant Spray (www.lafes.com)
- Naturally Fresh Deodorant Crystal Spray Mist (www.tccd.com)
- Solay Salt Stone (www.natural-salt-lamps.com)

DIAPER CREAM
- Carol's Daughter Unscented Body Jelly (www.carolsdaughter.com)
- Earth Mama-Angel Baby Bottom Balm (www.earthmamaangelbaby.com)
- Earth Tribe Kids Baby Balm (www.cosmeticsdatabase.com)
- Terressentials 100% Organic Terrific Tush Treatment (www.terressentials.com)

DIAPERS
- G Diapers Starter Kit (www.gdiapers.com)
- Huggies Pure and Natural (www.huggiespureandnatural.com)
- National Association of Diaper Services (www.diapernet.org)
- Organic Cotton Cloth Diapers (www.greennest.com)

DISHWASHING DETERGENT
- Biokleen with Natural Oxygen Bleach (www.bi-o-kleen.com)
- Ecover Tablets (www.ecover.com/us/en/Products/Dishes)

FACIAL CLEANSER
- CVS Facial Cleansing Pads (www.cvs.com)
- Nature's Plus Natural Beauty Cleansing Bar (www.naturesplus.com)

FEMININE HYGIENE
- The Diva Cup (www.divacup.com)
- Glad Rags (www.gladrags.com)
- Goddess Pads (www.goddesspads.com)
- Lunapads International (www.lunapads.com)
- The Keeper (www.keeper.com)

FLOORING
- 100% Natural, Bio-Degradable Carpets (www.earthweave.com)
- FLOR Recycled – Love Ewe, Lamb Cord, and Shaggy Sheep (www.flor.com)
- Forbo Flooring Systems Marmoleum Flooring (www.forboflooringna.com)
- Mohawk Carpet – Smartstrand and Everstrand (www.mohawkflooring.com/carpeting)

FOOD STORAGE
- Anchor Hocking Kitchen Storage Containers (www.anchorhocking.com)
- Bormioli Rocco Frigoverre Glass Storage Set (www.bormioliroccoprofessional.com)
- Corelle (www.corelle.com)
- Corningware (www.corningware.com)
- Kinetic Go Green Glasslock (www.kinetic-cookware.com)
- Preserve Plastic Storage Containers (www.preserveproducts.com)
- Pyrex (www.pyrexware.com)

FOUNDATION / POWDER
- Coastal Classic Creations Refreshing Mist Loose Powder (www.coastalclassiccreations.com)
- Jane Iredale Powder-Me (www.janeiredale.com)
- Rejuva Minerals Foundation (www.rejuvaminerals.com)
- Zosimos Botanicals (www.zosimosbotanicals.com)

FRAGRANCE
- Dancing Dingo Aromatherapy Blend (www.dancingdingo.com)
- Healing-Scents Naked Lavender Essential Oil (www.healing-scents.com)
- Mountain Girl Botanics – Essential Spritz Lavender Meadow (www.mountaingirlbotanics.com)
- Trillium Organics Botanical Perfume (www.trilliumorganics.com)

FURNACE FILTER
- 3M Filtrete Filters (www.3m.com/filtrete)

HAND SANITIZER
- EO Hand Sanitizing Spray (www.eoproducts.com)
- For My Kids Hand Wash (www.formykidsonline.com)
- Hand Sanz by All Terrain (www.allterrainco.com)
- Thieves Hand Sanitizer, Wipes, and Soap (www.secretofthieves.com)

HOLIDAY CARDS & GIFT WRAP
- Bloomin Flower Cards (www.bloomin.com)
- Earth Love'n Paper Products (www.earthloven.com)
- Nesting Shoppe (www.nestingshoppe.com)
- Pleasantrees (www.pleasantrees.com)
- Poopoopaper (www.poopoopaper.com)
- ReProduct (www.ReProduct.net)
- Wrapsacks (www.Wrapsacks.com)

HOME TESTING
- Do-it-Yourself Home Detox Green Toolbox (www.HomeDetoxGreenToolbox.com)

HOTELS
- Green/Environmentally-Friendly Hotels (www.environmentallyfriendlyhotels.com)
- The Green Hotels Association (www.greenhotels.com)

INK REFILL RESOURCE
- Refillable Ink Cartridges (Ex: HP, Lexmark, Epson, Canon) (www.theinkjetrefillstore.com)
- Walgreens (www.walgreens.com)

INSECT REPELLENT
- Burt's Bees Herbal Insect Repellent (www.burtsbees.com)
- Buzz Away Insect Repellent Spray or Towellettes (www.quantumhealth.com)

INSULATION
- The Ultratouch Multi-Purpose Roll Insulation (www.bondedlogic.com)
- Thermafleece (www.secondnatureuk.com)

JUNK MAIL, OPTING OUT
- 41pounds.org (www.41pounds.org)
- Catalog Choice (www.catalogchoice.org)
- Direct Marketing Association (www.DMAchoice.org)
- Stop the Junk Mail (www.stopthejunkmail.com)
- Tonic MailStopper (www.mailstopper.tonic.com)

LAUNDRY DETERGENT
- Ecos (www.ecos.com)
- Free and Clear Detergent (www.seventhgeneration.com)
- He Detergent (www.methodhome.com)
- Trader Joe's Laundry Detergent (www.traderjoes.com/locations.asp)

LIGHTING
- LED Waves (www.ledwaves.com)
- LEDbulb (www.ledbulb.com)
- Verilux Full Spectrum Lighting (www.verilux.com)

LUNCH BOXES
- Basura Bags (http://www.basurabags.org)
- Hero Bags (www.herobags.com)
- To-Go Ware Stainless Steel Lunch Containers and Carriers (www.to-goware.com)

MAKEUP
- Aubrey (www.aubrey-organics.com)
- Color Science (www.colorescience.com)
- Josie Maran (www.josiemarancosmetics.com)
- Juice Beauty (www.juicebeauty.com)
- ZuZu Luxe (www.gabrielcosmeticsinc.com)

MATTRESSES
- Moisture Pad (Organic Wool Moisture Pad available at www.suitesleep.com)
- Natural Rubber Organic Mattress (www.greennest.com)

MOP
- Method Omop (www.methodhome.com)

MOUTHWASH
- Healing Scents Mouthwash (www.healing-scents.com)
- Jäson Healthy Mouth Mouthwash Tea Tree and Cinnamon (www.jason-natural.com)

- Miessence Freshening Mouthwash
  (www.miorganicproducts.com)
- Tom's of Maine Mouthwash
  (www.tomsofmaine.com)

MOVING BOXES
- Rent-A-Green Box
  (www.earthfriendlymoving.com.)
- Used Cardboard Boxes
  (www.UsedCardboardBoxes.com)

NUT SPREADS
- Manitoba Harvest Hemp Seed Butter
  (www.manitobaharvest.com)
- Sunflower Seed Butter
  (www.sunbutter.com)

NUTRITION
- Integrative Nutrition Consultants, LLC
  (www.incnutrition.com)
- Perfectly Healthy Nutrition Products
  (www.perfectlyhealthy.net)

ORGANIZATIONS
- The American Council for an Energy-Efficient Economy (www.aceee.org)
- American Lung Association
  (www.lungusa.org)
- Asthma and Allergy Foundation of America (www.aafa.org)
- Beyond Pesticides
  (www.beyondpesticides.org)
- Environmental Defense Fund
  (www.edf.org/home.cfm)
- Environmental Media Association
  (www.ema-online.org)
- Environmental Working Group
  (www.ewg.org)
- Green America
  (www.greenamericatoday.org)
- Greenpeace USA
  (www.greenpeace.org/usa)
- Healthy Child Healthy World
  (www.Healthychildhealthyworld.com)
- Institute for Bau-Biologie & Ecology
  (www.buildingbiology.net)
- The Nature Conservancy
  (www.nature.org)
- Organic Consumers Association
  (www.organicconsumers.org)
- Safe Cosmetics Action Network
  (www.safecosmetics.org)
- Sierra Club (www.sierraclub.org)

OVENS
- Global Sun Oven (www.sunoven.com)

PACKING MATERIALS
- PaperNuts (www.papernuts.com)
- Staples Biodegradable Packing Peanuts
  (www.staples.com)

PAIN REMEDIES
- Sumbody Zappers (www.sumbody.com)

PAINT

- AFM Safecoat Zero VOC Flat Paint (www.afmsafecoat.com)
- Benjamin Moore Natural Paint (www.benjaminmoore.com)
- Dunn Edwards Eco Shield Zero VOC Paint (www2.dunnedwards.com)
- Sherwin Williams Zero VOC Paint Harmony (www.sherwin-williams.com)
- Zero VOC Mythic Paint (www.mythicpaint.com)

PAPER TOWELS

- Earth Friendly (www.ecos.com)
- Marcal Paper (www.marcalpaper.com)
- Seventh Generation (www.seventhgeneration.com)

PEST CONTROL

- Extreme Bug Vac (www.amazon.com)
- Beyond Pesticides (www.beyondpesticides.org)

PETS

DOG TOYS

- Simply Fido Pet Toys (www.simplyfido.com)

DOG WASTE BAGS

- Bio Bags Dog Waste Bags (www.biobagusa.com)

PET BED

- Green Nest Organic Pet Bed (www.GreenNest.com)

PET DEODORIZER

- S.A.M Zer-Odor Reducer (www.petdiscounters.com)
- Worlds Best Cat Litter (www.worldsbestcatlitter.com)

PET FOOD

- The Honest Kitchen (Verve, Embark) (www.thehonestkitchen.com)
- Newman's Own Organics Premium Pet Foods (www.newmansownorganics.com)
- Pet Promise Dog Food (www.petpromiseinc.com)

PHONE BOOKS DELIVERY

- Phone Company – Value Conscious (Credo Mobile (www.credomobile.com)
- Yellow Pages – Stop the Delivery of Telephone Books (www.yellowpagesgoesgreen.org)

PILLOW COVERS

- Allersoft Certified Organic Pillow Cover (www.amazon.com)
- Green Nest Organic Cotton Barrier Cover (www.greennest.com)
- Green Sleep Natural Rubber Pillow (www.greensleep.ca/pdf/greensleep_brochure.pdf)

RECYCLING RESOURCES

- Earth 911 (www.Earth911.org)

- Freecycle.org (www.FREECYCLE.ORG)
- Recycle Bank (www.recyclebank.com)

CARPET
- Carpet America Recovery Effort
  (www.carpetrecovery.org)

CELL PHONE
- Cell for Cash (www.CellforCash.com)
- Cell Phones for Soldiers
  (www.cellphonesforsoldiers.com)
- CollectiveGood Mobile Phone Recycling
  (www.collectivegood.com)
- Eco-Cell (www.eco-cell.com)
- ReCellular (www.recellular.com)
- Wireless Recycling
  (www.wirelessrecycling.com)
- Call 2 Recycle (www.call2recycle.org)

ELECTRONICS
- Costco Trade-In & Recycle
  (www.costco.gazelle.com)
- Recycle Old Electronics
  (www.recycle4free.net)
- Ink Cartridges
- Castle Ink (www.CastleInk.com)

SHOES
- Nike's Reuse a Shoe
  (www.nikereuseashoe.com)

SHAMPOO
- MGA Shampoo
  (www.maxgreenalchemy.com)
- Solay Unscented Green Tea
  Shampoo/Body Bar
  (www.natural-salt-lamps.com)
- Healing Scents Shampoo
  (healing-scents.com)

SHAVING CREAM
- Aubrey Organics Creme de la Shave
  (www.aubrey-organics.com)
- Dr. Bronner's Magic Baby Shaving Gel
  (www.drbronner.com)
- Tom's of Maine Shave Cream
  (www.tomsofmaine.com)

SHOPPING BAGS
- A Better Bag
  (www.wholefoodsmarket.com)
- Bag-E-Wash & Dryer
  (www.bag-e-wash.com)
- Trader Joe's Plastic Bottle Bag
  (www.traderjoes.com)
- Reusablebags.com
  (www.reusablebags.com)
- Whole Foods Recycled Foldable Tote
  (www.wholefoodsmarket.com)

SHOPPING GUIDES
- Blue Ocean Institute Text for Safer Fish
  Alternatives (www.fishphone.org)
- Clean Air-Cool Planet Consumer Guide
  (www.cleanair-coolplanet.org)
- Consumer Reports / Greener Sources
  (http://www.greenerchoices.org)

Shopping Guides continued
- Environmental Defense Fund's Seafood Selector (www.edf.org)
- Food News, a Project of Environmental Working Group (www.foodnews.org)
- The Green Office (www.thegreenoffice.com)
- Green Office Tips (www.The9to5Greened.com)
- Greenpeace "The Guide to Greener Electronics" (www.greenpeace.org)
- Handy Guide for Pet Shopping (www.petsfortheenvironment.org)
- Natural Resources Defense Council – Seafood Scorecard (nrdc.org/health/effects/mercury/walletcard.pdf)
- Organic Consumers Association (www.organicconsumers.org)
- Printer Ink and Toner Price Comparison (www.inkguides.com)
- Skin Deep (www.cosmeticsdatabase.com)
- You Home Through Green-Colored Glasses (www.GreenColoredGlasses.net)

SHOWER FAUCETS AND FILTERS
- Aquasana Chlorine and Thh Reduction (www.aquasanastore.com)
- Lowes Faucet Aerators & Low Flow Shower Heads (www.lowes.com)

SKIN CARE
- Arcona Skin Care (www.arcona.com)
- Dr. Alkaitis (www.alkaitis.com)
- Sircuit Skin (www.sircuitskin.com)

SLEEPWEAR
- Green Nest (http://www.greennest.com)

SOLAR
- Hymini/Mini Solar (www.hymini.com)
- Kinesis K3 Wind and Solar Charger (www.kinesisindustries.com)
- Solar Cell Phone Charger (www.solio.com)
- Solar Home Heliostats (www.practicalsolar.com)

SUNSCREEN
- Badger Sunscreen, SPF 30 (www.badgerbalm.com)
- California Baby Sunblock Stick No Fragrance, SPF 30+ (www.californiababy.com)
- Jane Iredale Powder-Me, SPF Dry Sunscreen, SPF 30 (www.janeiredale.com)
- Jäson's Mineral Based Physical Sunblock SPF 30+ (www.jason-natural.com)
- Keys Soap Solar Rx Cosmetic Sunblock, SPF 30 (www.keys-soap.com)
- Soleo Sunscreen Organic Chemical-Free Sunscreen SPF 30+ (www.soleousa.com)
- Trukid Sunny Days Facestick SPF 30+

Mineral Sunscreen, UVA/UVB Broad Spectrum (trukid.com)

SWEETENER

- 100% Organic Agave Nectar (www.wildorganics.net)
- Stevia (www.sweetleaf.com)

THERMOSTATS

- Honeywell Programmable Thermostats (www.honeywell-thermostat.com)

TOILET TISSUE

- Earth Friendly Products (www.ecos.com)
- Green Forest (www.greenforest-products.com)
- Marcal's Small Steps (www.marcalpaper.com)
- Seventh Generation (www.seventhgeneration.com)

TOOTHPASTE

- Burt's Bees Children's Toothpaste (www.burtsbees.com)
- Kiss My Face Aloedyne Toothpaste (www.kissmyface.com)
- Peelu Toothpaste (www.peelu.com)
- Tom's of Maine Natural Antiplaque Toothpaste (www.tomsofmaine.com)

TOYS

- Green Toys (www.GreenToys.com)
- Haba – Wooden First Blocks (www.blueberryforest.com)
- Hazelnut Kids (www.hazelnutkids.com)
- Organic Plush Toys from Miyim Simple Organic Toys (www.miyim.com)
- Toy Testing (www.HealthyToys.org)

TRAVEL – BUSINESS CONFERENCES

- Skype Software (www.skype.com)
- Travel Food (Laptop Lunch (www.laptoplunches.com)

VACATIONS

- Home Base Holidays (www.homebase-hols.com)
- Home Exchange (HomeExchange.com)

VACUUMS AND ACCESSORIES

- 3M Filtrete Bags, Belts, and Filters (www.filtretevac.com)
- Kenmore Progressive 35922 (www.kenmore.com)
- Hoover Wind Tunnel Anniversary Edition U6485-900 (www.hoover.com)
- The Versatility by Electrolux (www.electroluxusa.com)

VALENTINE'S DAY

- Chocolatl's Raw Chocolate Sauce (www.flowfoodschocolatl.com)
- Dagoba Chocolate (www.dagobachocolate.com)
- Global Exchange Chocolate Assortments (www.globalexchangestore.org)

Valentine's Day continued
- Organic Bouquet
  (www.Organicbouquet.com)

WATER BOTTLES
- Intak Hydration Bottle
  (www.thermos.com)
- Klean Kanteen (www.kleankanteen.com)
- Think Sport (www.thinksportbottles.com)

WATER FILTERS, DISTILLERS, REVERSE OSMOSIS
- Brita Aqualux Carafe (www.brita.com/us)
- Pur Horizontal Fm9400 Faucet Mount
  (www.purwaterfilter.com)
- Reverse Osmosis Water Filtration
  (http://www.greennest.com)
- Waterwise Distiller (www.waterwise.com)

WATER HEATERS
- GE Water Heaters
  (www.geappliances.com)

WEDDINGS
Charities
- Charitable Invitations
  (www.idofoundation.org)
- Justgive Online Charitable Giving
  (www.JustGive.org)
Favors
- Organic Wedding Favors
  (www.chocolatebar.com)
Gowns
- Buy or Sell Wedding Gowns
  (www.preownedweddingdresses.com)
- New and Preowned Wedding Items
  (www.bravobride.com)
Invitations
- Grow-A-Note Cards
  (www.greenfieldpaper.com)
- Bloom Handmade Paper
  (www.bloompaperproducts.com)
- Greenfield Wedding Invitations
  (www.greenfiledpaper.com)
Rings
- Brilliant Earth Conflict-Free Diamonds
  (www.brilliantearth.com)
- Greenkarat (www.greenkarat.com)
- Polar Bear Diamond
  (www.polarbeardiamond.com)
- Certified Conflict-Free Diamonds
  (www.conflictfreediamonds.org)

WINE
- Bonterra Organic Wine
  (www.bonterra.com)
- Sterling Organic Wine
  (www.sterlingvineyards.com)

WORKSHOPS
- Eco Nest (www.econest.com)
- Green Nest Seminars
  (www.GreenNest.com)
- Yestermorrow Design/Build School's
  "Biofuels" Workshop
  (www.yestermorrow.org)

PHOTO CREDITS

All photos from or by Hollan Publishing unless otherwise noted.

Page 10: Preserve by Recycline
Page 68: Courtesy of Suite Sleep, Inc.
Page 94: Courtesy of Green Nest LLC
Page 98: Courtesy of Topway Global, Inc.
Page 114: Courtesy of Used Cardboard Boxes, Inc.
Page 142: Courtesy of Hosung NY Trading Inc.
Page 148: Courtesy of Suite Sleep, Inc.
Page 158: Courtesy of Hosung NY Trading Inc.
Page 214: Courtesy of *Sum*body LLC
Page 224: Courtsey of Laptop Lunches
Page 279: Courtesy of Zion Judaica

ABOUT THE AUTHORS

LISA AND RON BERES are the founders of *www.GreenNest.com*, Certified Green Building Professionals (CGBP), and Certified Building Biology Environmental Consultants (BBECs). They are the authors of the audio CDs *Learn to Create a Healthy Home!, The 9 to 5 Greened,* and *Your Home Through Green Colored Glasses.* Lisa is the author of the children's book, *My Body My House.* They have appeared on Fox *and Friends, The Today Show with Matt Lauer, Chelsea Lately, The Doctors, Living Well with Montel Williams,* and Discovery's Planet Green show *Greenovate.* Lisa has been a guest on Martha Stewart Living Radio and is a regular green correspondent for the Sally Jessy Raphael radio show. The consulting business includes celebrities like Trista Sutter (ABC's *The Bachelorette*) as well as Fortune 1000 companies. They live in the Los Angeles area. Please visit them at www. GreenNest.com.

> As human beings, our greatness lies not so much
> in being able to remake the world—that is the myth of
> the atomic age—as in being able to remake ourselves.
>
> — MAHATMA GANDHI